William Entriken Baily

Classical Poems

William Entriken Baily

Classical Poems

ISBN/EAN: 9783744651912

Printed in Europe, USA, Canada, Australia, Japan

Cover: Foto ©Thomas Meinert / pixelio.de

More available books at **www.hansebooks.com**

BY

WILLIAM ENTRIKEN BAILY.

> *Hoc est
> Vivere bis, vitâ posse priore frui.*
> — MARTIAL.

PRESS OF
ROBERT CLARKE & CO.
CINCINNATI, O
1892.

Copyright, 1891, by WILLIAM ENTRIKEN BAILY.

PREFACE.

It may be well to refer to some of the conditions by which the essential number of the poems in this book has been produced. Though they are not all classical in subjects, yet those that are not are often classical in spirit, as well as lyrical. They owe their origin first, to temperamental characteristics; secondly, to the animus of a great deal of what constitutes orthodox English poetry, as found in the pages of SHAKESPEARE, MILTON, COLLINS, KEATS, WORDSWORTH and TENNYSON, with, perhaps, influences at work from SHELLEY and his school. The undercurrent of meaning of the poems, in many cases, is didactic, as much so (if not more) as certain passages in SPENSER'S "Fairy Queen." It has been shown by eminent critics on both sides of the Atlantic that this is a false principle in the art of verse; on the contrary, it has been shown by other eminent critics that it is a true one. If a reader of an epic feels that its strain, its intellectual tenor, its grouping of noble characters for instructive effects, its subtle agreements with the finer elements of civilization perpetually in play (that have been taught the author by the philosophers, moralists and theologians of his time), and the occasional free display of them in the course of the story, are of the didactic kind, his feelings must certainly be a judge to himself in the matter, but not to others. His emotions naturally appropriate to themselves what supports the nature of their instincts, this nature having perhaps an entirely different bias in another reader, and thus the two are unable to feel and see in a like manner, not only in the perusal of an epic, but also of a drama at its best. Two able readers, of unlike bent in appreciation, may write in combination a critique on an epic, and do it justice; but it often takes four to write one on a drama with the same result, because the elements in it are of a more complex order.

It inclines, even in its tragic form, to the pleasurable in a more obvious way. Notwithstanding that SHAKESPEARE represents the spirit of the troubadour in his plays—plays most especially addressed to the courtiers, the pedants, the pleasure-seekers and the men-about-town of his day—the didactic, mingled with the real and the ideal, is frequently presenting itself; notably in his aphorisms, in his numerous outlines suggesting the moral artist, in his use of what is called poetic justice, in his ethical tendencies as a whole (above those of other dramatists of his time), and in his sense of responsibility to the higher consciousness of humanity. In JOHN MILTON we find the spirit of the Puritan—a spirit that easily adjusted itself to what is harsh and doctrinal in life and religion, for the scholastic spirit to take up and form into a long narrative poem of undoubted didactic type. He was too much of a scholar and a man of genius not to know the value of art in clothing his doctrines as a mere thinker of common experience; and he was too much of a scholar and a man of fine instincts not to know the value of SHAKESPEARE to other mere thinkers of the doctrinal class would they but see him through the eye of scholarship. His lines to the great dramatist are in this respect very significant. We thus see in SPENSER the didactic is a controlling principle; in SHAKESPEARE it is an occasional, but still a manifest principle; and in JOHN MILTON it is, as with SPENSER, a controlling principle. Coming down to WORDSWORTH, we find it a settled principle with him, his name alone suggesting virtue, honor, reverence, duty, love, humility, honest poverty, time and fate, abstract qualities holding an ever varying relation through his muse to the strictest rules of didactics in prosaic life. If a philosophical sect were now formed after the manner of some of those of the ancients, having in view the mere teaching of moral laws, it would without a doubt derive much help, not only from WORDSWORTH, but also from many of his poetical contemporaries and successors in point of time who have the beautiful before them, yet who show, unconsciously, a presence—a main idea or a stray idea—in their poems akin to the inculcation of a precept or precepts. The love of certain higher attributes in man leads to an idealization of them in statuary and painting; and to say that poetry of the beautiful should ignore such attributes, is to say that it is inferior in its mission to statuary and painting—is to ascribe to it an inherent tone of weakness—is to charge it with inability to embody with itself the fact that this age is pre-eminently didactic in its drift. As for the successful expression of the beautiful, with its impalpable essence, no other century, not excepting the Elizabethan era, equals the present one in its list of poems. Such writers as KEATS, SHELLEY and TENNYSON have given to the English-speaking world examples in this respect very difficult to surpass. The poet-laureate, in particular, has an influence over his readers through a mastered craft that sublimates whatever it touches, and that tends to add to their perceptions of the noble and to broaden their existence in a wise way. In this regard, and in others, he takes a decided superiority over either SHELLEY or KEATS, and holds strong connections with WORDSWORTH and MILTON, also with SPENSER in an esthetic way. It thus can be seen the system of poetry has for one of its prime resources the didactic, infusing into its work, as it does, elements of usefulness, reality and strength. A moral meaning may be presented so as to impress its purpose too emphatically; then it tends not to high art—it tends to utility for utility's sake—to the ground where prose wears the mask of rhyme. In a true poem, some essential fact of life, the soul of the piece, reveals itself in an unity of details, the fact losing itself apparently in the details at times, but in its impression as a whole it is effective in inducing a frame of mind in the reader more favorable to its cause than in a single rigorous disclosure of itself. In this case the charm and the lesson go hand-in-hand, and the Powers that rule over the destiny of poetry are generally satisfied.

In offering these explanations, it is with no desire to make certain ideas in a matter of art obtrusive, but with a desire to supply information that in its absence might make the poems herein printed seem to be without a key, holding as they do relations to English literature of a kind indicated.   W. E. B.

INDEX TO POEMS.

	PAGE.
Prelude	9
The Queen of Dreamland	11
The Hero and the Wife	20
Horace	28
The Choice of Alcides	34
The City in Ruins	42
Down Amid the Shadows	46
The Plato of the Town	49
The Recluse	53
The Insistence of Nature	56
Tempus Fugit	59
Stepping-Stones	63
Sleep	70
Old Age	72
Beauty	74
Aurora	76
Adversity	79
Fate and Prophecy	80
May	80
The Sybarite	81
The Birth of Venus	83
Pomona	85
My Lady	87
At Sea	89
The Caged Bird	91
The Royal Road	93
The Appian Way	95
The Statue	97
The Island	101
Before and After the Voyage	107

PRELUDE.

WHAT blissfulness 't would be Apollo's lyre
To hear at June's bright dawn, by night's star-fire,
   As come and go life's vagaries! Replete
   With sounds that charm would be the matchless feat
To form web-works of tone! The high-born choir,
Who sing through time, whose harmonies inspire
   Fancy's ardency, aspiration meet,
   Courage, nobleness, sympathies concrete,
How they seem demi-gods! Them modify
   Hope's own art ever breathing in control,
She through them speaking; for each death-dull eye
   She wakes, bids lips partake from her strange bowl,
Emboldens hands to strive, man's strength to ply
   To gain the power that was Apollo's soul.

CLASSICAL POEMS.

THE QUEEN OF DREAMLAND.

I.

I DREAMED.—Venus approached with languid air.
   More near she seemed as one full meet to dwell
In ideal realms encrowned with honors rare
   'Mong Fancy's spirits deemed ineffable;
Yet made her footsteps prints upon the sand;
They proved a being true of Day's Dreamland.

II.

A palace stood anear; it was a pile
   That covered acres with majestic weight;
Its marble art was of a simple style;
   On roofs were domes, each with an ancient trait,
As gleaming roses swayed in urns anear,
And odored well the summer atmosphere.

III.

Had outlooks wide high windows here and there
   Upon green dales and distant mountain points;
Portals the facade graced with arches rare,
   Their brazen hinges shining in the joints;
Long porticos there stood that mildly shed
Their column-shades on steps that upward spread.

IV.

Venus moved on with head inclining low,
  Nearing a portal dark. She was alone;
She mused, and feared awhile within to go;
  The deep, dim hall with kind and welcome tone
No entrance bade—'t was as a dismal dell
Repulsed her with a strange, foreboding spell.

V.

She onward moves ere long; stops in amaze;
  Harkens as if she saw with startled ken;
Observes the pictured walls, great clouds ablaze
  With Jove's stern darts hurled from his thund'rous den;
But soon she drops her maiden veil of fears,
And bears a courage of a matron's years.

VI.

Anon she treads a stairway, thence to pass
  Into a hall before. Herein salutes
The eye a bright display of central glass—
  On ceiling broad a dome. Sol mildly shoots
Enkindling gleams through panes, with emblems spread,
That show what might to vesper orbs is wed.

VII.

Ceilings of cedar wood adorn the place
  (Contrived with skill to show the artist's dye),
Whereon true genius has depicted grace
  In figures formed Jove's dreams to glorify.
Floating bubbles are borne from cherubs fair,
As others range with self-oblivious air.

VIII.

Below are pendent apples o'er a stream
   Upon a tree all silver-wet with dew;
And from bent boughs fall to the current's gleam,
   The heaviest the cherubs by to woo;
These see the fruitage swimming in the tide,
And vie to gather up the best espied.

IX.

She marks about the statue-figures spread
   Upon the floor. Anon her breath is slow;
She feels as if she from herself has fled
   And soul-fit mysteries upon her flow;
It is so rare to gaze and be unknown
Among such shapes endowed with subtile tone.

X.

Ere long she leaves behind the spell-like hall,
   And gains a distant aisle, egress to make;
Her silent footsteps move beside a wall
   Massive with stones too firm for Time to shake;
A winding passage guides toward a court,
Where fowls tame-bred and mortal forms consort.

XI.

A tranquil court it is wherein a bird
   Might lull itself to sleep at warm mid-day;
Where marble brims reflecting baths engird
   Under cool canopies; where alcoves gay
Hold forth soft seats on which young drowsy Thought
Can range in Dreamland with old romance fraught.

XII.

About the open space irregular
  Rise roof-crowned walls, whose shades unite with shades;
Nor do below they noontide gleams debar
  From touching marble steps to long arcades;
A just degree of light and shade controls,
And with mild means the atmosphere consoles.

XIII.

Above is seen a row of galleries,
  Where curtains white, wind-blown, exhibit faces
And hands embroidering; deep balconies,
  With tiers of shelves on which are Grecian vases,
Whose plant o'er plant have colors fresh and gay,
Like pageantry of Fairyland's display.

XIV.

The turtle-dove about the court is seen
  To hover here and there with wings broadspread;
A peacock bright expands his plumage green,
  Admiration to gain from folks ahead;
And 'mong all those he meets reclining by
No scorn upon a brow he can descry.

XV.

Venus three doves beholds. They near her oft
  Fly with capricious yet regardful ways;
As prudent bees around June's bushes soft
  Dally before they settle on their sprays,
So one by one the birds steal down to rest
And breathe a welcome on the stranger-guest.

XVI.

The folks first see her by a pillar's shade;
   Murmurs besiege her ear; from doorways nigh
Come comrade-forms with those from some arcade;
   About her gather all; part to apply
Numerous queries, handing back her words
To outer heads whose eagerness engirds.

XVII.

She not reluctant leads them to inquire
   About a realm afar, with civic din
Of man disturbed; about a monarch's ire
   Whose laws unjust stand much opposed. To win
Their sympathy, she meekly then alludes
Unto herself, and o'er a sorrow broods.

XVIII.

The monarch with a strange and mad uproar
   Had made her breast of late to dolor prone;
Had scowled and grudged her rights; and now no more
   She cares to dwell at home until had flown
A time of pilgrimage, when smoothly laid
Might be his rage with reason's sober aid.

XIX.

Her guileless story has a mellow power
   To place deep confidence in every heart;
Each excellence of mind becomes her dower
   Viewed through the glamor of befriending art;
And all her hearers to warm fancies yield,
That hint of much in her heart's depth concealed.

XX.

At last the folks disperse; with ling'ring throb
    They muse; and as slow-rolling drops of dew
Unite (and from themselves their forms do rob)
    With fellow-ones upon a violet blue,
So emotions unite, with zeal o'errun,
And swell to bounds from various bosoms won.

XXI.

Unto meek Venus they with tongues serene
    Due homage pay. Anon expressions flow
To favor her with prestige of a queen,
    On her a gentle weight of glory throw;
They feel she is a ruler to maintain
The honors of a future golden reign.

XXII.

Before to them she was a mere surmise;
    To life most real she is committed now—
Transfigured all!—a being claiming ties
    With ideal worlds, thus gifted to endow
A multitude of souls in Day's Dreamland,
Busy with deeds, with inner guidance grand.

XXIII.

At last at twilight hour courtiers reveal
    To her their purpose, saying that awaits
For her a sceptered right to rule their weal,
    Abating from themselves superior traits
With urbane art in order to make less
Seem to herself her own unworthiness.

XXIV.

A bard steps forth, his visage grave and old;
   Long locks of white upon his shoulders roll;
His minstrel-hand is oft inspired to hold
   The harp to notes concordant with the soul;
His voice ascending o'er the swaying heads
Softly entreats and warm impressions spreads.

XXV.

Venus confused with much ado demurs;
   Resorts to argument to help her cause;
Unto her budding youth she next refers;
   This failing, she aloof alone withdraws;
Some follow her; she tries with words to foil;
But their deep love she doth with sense entoil.

XXVI.

They urge with courteous tact; some call her cold,
   Augment their accents low with fertile fears;
Their melancholy shades increase two-fold;
   Feelings acute express themselves in tears;
All move engirdled by a magic spell,
On whose sweet cause they fondly, strangely dwell.

XXVII.

They tell her of a prophet who had told
   That she would come at last to be their queen;
That Truth in league with Beauty, as of old,
   Was moving still toward a future scene,
To triumph o'er the world's debarring years,
Ties to divulge 'tween this and higher spheres.

XXVIII.

Venus in time, with motive half aware
  Of self, consents. Assuming honors new
With chiding doubt, bemasks a pallor rare
  The roses of her cheek. She trembles through
As tongues the tidings bear. Now won the cause,
The court resounds with clamor and applause.

XXIX.

What happiness betrays each eager face!
  Sweet flutes play on! Ye instruments more gay,
Breathe all your harmony about the place!
  Meek Venus now retires and fades away
To wait to-morrow's ceremonial grand;
Therefore, glad tones, your utmost skill expand!

XXX.

To-morrow comes. In dome-crowned hall appear
  A noble throng beside a purple throne;
A semi-circle vast of people near;
  Behind them maidens rare, all sweetly known
(As blushes on their cheeks most softly charm)
To youths hard by, with badges on each arm.

XXXI.

Some boys confront Venus upon the throne;
  Each holds a silver harp of fervent strings,
Revealing limitations of its tone,
  That bears itself abroad on waning wings;
And—sweet succession!—they a hymn well chant,
Those minstrel-boys in robes, so jubilant!

XXXII.

A score of matrons come in vestments white
　　Adown an aisle with grace; each duly shows
A homage fit the ceremonial rite;
　　They onward move to honored seats in rows;
Ascends forthwith the hymn's assuaging chant
From minstrel-boys in robes, so jubilant!

XXXIII.

Come next a score of elder-men, arrayed
　　In cloaks of black; a leader bears a wreath
(That soon before the throne is lowly laid);
　　They turn to seats the glowing dome beneath;
Ascends forthwith the hymn's assuaging chant
From minstrel-boys in robes, so jubilant!

XXXIV.

Some gleaner-girls in singing then proceed
　　To glorify their task with duteous voice,
Addressed to pow'rs above their aid to plead,
　　As all their shining faces well rejoice;
Full gratified they rest like sea-shell low,
Who's found its pearl within dark surges' flow.

XXXV.

Venus they then approach; upon her head
　　A simple laurel-crown bestows a hand,
And throngs on throngs a speechless blessing shed
　　Upon the maiden Queen of Day's Dreamland,
Pleading that she with them may long abide
To rule their weal until Death's eventide.

XXXVI.

Then vows by mortal breasts ascending go;
  Adopt they aims for their alloted days
Befit true hearts, subjecting flesh full low
  To serve a spirit high, that Truth may raise
A guardian o'er each golden life that far
Its worth may shine a clear, enduring star.

XXXVII.

Ere long a show'r falls on the outer court,
  But passes soon away; and mildly then
A rainbow gay with omen comes athwart,
  Copious seasons foretelling to the ken;
And all to future years their faces turn,
An epoch rich and Beauty there discern.

THE HERO AND THE WIFE.

HE was a Roman of superior form.
  The moment now was come wherein to choose
This way or that. Distrust prevailed in him,
Disturbing homebred sentiments, like hawks
In orchard causing happy birds of song
Anxiety. Habit restrained him, too,
In such a course as now therefrom to break
Was hard. Yet with an introspective eye
He saw his tone of self had epic warmth,
By which it would inspire heroic zeal
To be a conqueror with trophied trains.

The discordance that was within himself
(As to and fro he swayed among armed men)
Could not endure annoyance from the hums
About, when it would have a tranquil hour
Or so to calm and veer from doubt to hope.
But as the sun forth shone 'tween clouds, from it
Influence came, instilling him with aught
Obscure, profound, transferring by degrees
Him from that which he scorned to that which he
Aspired, as through himself emotions moved
Assured. Referring to ideals of life,
Long cherished by his memory, he found
An essence in them all sustaining them
With beauty and its pow'r and mystery
Too deep for man.

     Anon he spoke : "The gods
Demand my services, my country asks
For them upon the tented field, and comes
An inspiration moving me to go
Rewards to have. For earthly dignity
And crown celestial yearn I tacitly;
If victor in the battle's cause, the first
Is mine, whilst living to enjoy; if slain,
The gods approving, faith doth prophesy
The second's mine. Here linger I and pine
And older grow, the days fulfilling not
What me should gratify. Fortune hath led
Unto satiety in zigzag paths;
She made no sacrifice to Happiness;

To follow her is sacrilege. My joys—
Domestic joys—my wife and I, espoused
Like April odors fresh to April hues—
Are faded now. They blossomed forth, then bore
Sweet fruit, which, tasting o'er and o'er, soon cloyed
Desire, yet left me hungry for the meat
That does not come. 'Tis starving nature roused
That would its stay go seek. Nuptial ties
Appear entangling by the charm that comes
From action in a freer life abroad.
In changes we attain another self.
With will consenting, then impelling us,
'Tis we subserve the ends of destiny,
In concord with the mighty ones of yore,
Who strove along, conquering with an aim
That found a life through war which few lives know,
And fame historic afterwards."

       Anon
Calling for what the leader of a host
Would need, he strode among assembling men,
Breast-plated, ready warfare soon to face.
They felt that he, their haughty chief, kept step
With a pulsation true of what was brave,
Stern in an experience with the world.

 His wife came slowly forth; surveying him
She stood, impressing not as she was wont
With beauty and emotions that disarm
Men of their wills; but as a woman sees

A woman with an eye that dreads and hates,
Ashamed to own that it not trusts and loves—
So he saw her. Embarrassment o'ercame
Her by degrees, in her arousing doubts
Foreboding vaguely, then inspiring her
With energy to chide her lord, sullen,
Acting as if a stranger to herself.

She was to him the being of his choice,
Beside her proud; away, his sweeter part
Much missed. Chosen ardently, despite
Himself, nature propelling him to woo
With modesty, he now first since their day
Of wedlock vows, withstood her otherwise.
She plead to him with eloquence. He heard
As if to yield to what she asked, in brief
Disdain of what he felt before, but made
No answer. She then tried to win with gifts
The heart pays to the mind; but soon her voice
Prattled, not reasoned, and aroused his mien
Of cynicism, beholding her so void
As not to know him strong, but as him weak—
Shaming his lofty self with truthfulness.
Yet he to her was strength. A purpose frail
In her, a purpose resolute in him,
Were two, supporting and supported, yet
Were one in common sympathy that worked
In married harmony. For a brief while
She felt the tie was strained and he the cause,

And was to snap asunder soon. Then she
With other words with pensive thoughts thus spoke:

    "Oh, list, my lord! remain with me. What's life
With thee away? Let others to the war,
Less worthy living, dying worthy more;
Thy worth maintains itself where'er it is;
But theirs not so. Departing hence, thy gain
Is naught, thy loss domestic bliss. Then cease
Thy warfare with thyself; it makes me feel
Thy peril with a woman's fear, not man's,
And be a husband to thy wife again."

    He looked askance. Silence prevailed, and ere
Its power waned, he moved in coldness wrapped,
Seeing with mental eye some inner thing
That him absorbed. The moments passing by
Kept her in trembles of suspense; each was
So intermingled with mistrust it seemed
An hour of punishment. At last he turned
And said: "Why waitest thou?"

                           She bowed and wept,
Such visions playing in her mind as fear
Provokes in frailty. Yet it was a grief
Tempered; controlling moods unsettled much,
It made her prudent in her selfishness—
Her source of tears. Looking at him ere long,
The semblance of her husband in a form
Made bold appeared, who still retaining her

As his heart's paragon—none else for him—
A nobler self revealed, as slowly came
A spell that to her intuition showed
The solemn tenor of true thought in life
Inspiring him. A conscious rapture spread
Throughout her pulse in thinking such a one
Was closest to her bosom's rare desire,
And changed her nature higher likes to know.

 Turning he said: "Thou smilest through thy tears!
But late thy head did hang, lack-lustre was
Thy glance, and diffident thy manners were!
Yet presto!—a change!—thy woe wept tears,
But now thy joy weeps tears. Perplexes me
Thy fickleness; it breaks the link that should
Unite my comprehension to thyself.—
But let such matters go! To comfort thee,
My wife, the hero's motive ill consorts
With what the husband's tenderness would say;
Therefore, me understand, not by that which
I seem, but by that which I am, no words
Asking for than from me now comes."

       Futile
His speech; for she anticipating him,
Did feel what he wished her to feel—through love,
A knowledge of himself with lofty pow'rs
In visible relief. His traits more coarse,
O'ertopping hers, knew not the part she was

Unto his flesh, her flesh, in that her mind
Was subtile, his was dull.

                                    "Lately I would
Have said, Oh, hard thee to relinquish! Now,
Thy purpose moves in me, and makes me say
Thy choice of duty reason cheers, and makes
Me apt in sacrifice thy absence hence
To bear with a stout will," thus uttered she,
Deriving added strength from her good lord.

    Working upon his feelings with a fresh
Congenial mien—with woman's artless skill
Expressing estimation for himself,
And love behind it—stood they face to face,
The hero still supreme, yet softened some,
Slowly descending to the husband's plane,
Her patience helping him. Now free to use
Her will, his nature through with hers refined
Instilled she with sagacious joyousness,
Such as to feel a philosopher turns.

    He pressed her to his lips, then backwards stood,
Observing her as if with reverence,
Unapt to vent what he would say. At last
He spoke: "Before we part, I to the war,
Thou to the loom, to wishes list in thy
Behalf: I would have thee forever live
In simple happiness, to household things

THE HERO AND THE WIFE.

Attending, leaving duties that were mine
To manly hands; I would have thee, if low
I fall, remember me more in thy heart
Than in thy mind; I would have ever fresh
Thy dews of life in glory of the dawn;
Thy flow'rs of hope to grow with hues perfumed,
Thee bidding them; the fruit of our two loves
To bear the seed with aught, as ages pass,
Endowing fame on the parental stock,
Transplanted then to regions god-ruled o'er."

    He ceased, and not a murmur rose from throa's
Of men hard by, his followers—silence
Impressive reigned an interval, that he
Alone broke with a sigh. Then he, erect,
With chieftan airs, assumed command of them,
Now forming into ranks, and off all moved,
They seeming cold as statues, hills anon
Obscuring them, and distance hushing sounds
Of trumpet more and more until they died.

    Meanwhile the wife gazed into prospects far
Whither he had gone, feeling many things
That woman only knows. Yet with a heart
Encouraged she consoled a matron's mind,
Thinking no more of him as one far gone,
Mayhaps a captive chained—a galley slave—
A corse and stretched among the chariots' wreck;—
But as a patriot faithful to a cause;
A conqueror severe, yet merciful;

A hero coming from ovations fresh,
Loaded with spoils and emblems gained, the hum
Of heralds him before to tell the tale—
Fulfillment honored had endeavors brave.

'Twas thus to war he went on Roman soil,
And striving won, not by denying self
Examples to the mind of what was great,
But by a timely use of them.

HORACE.

I.

HORACE, thou scribe of yore!—what wisdom taught
    Thy methods slow!—how well at times indeed
Couldst thou passions console unduly fraught
    With yearnings false for fickle Fortune's meed!
Although of pagan creed, yet was thy mind
Accordant with the truth as then defined.

II.

Among thy Sabine fields, where beat Time's heart
    As even now, imparting to the frame
Of things a warmth occult which made them start
    Into outlines that reached ere blight their aim,
How breathed thy harp those sounds that not as yet
Have reached an end to pay a mortal debt!

III.

They breathe content, attended by a charm,
  Impressing bosoms with a happy thrill.
No sudden woes within can do much harm
  If minds forlorn yield to thy Orphean skill.
What was to thee thy life's most humble share?—
What was to thee the daunt in Fortune's air?

IV.

Exemplar thou, O schoolman in the dark!
  Thy praise of Poverty, her wholesome store,
Was worthy of thy philosophic ark,
  That on a flood of years a species bore
To live—consigning to an English soil
The true origins of thy midnight oil.

V.

Now these origins, much increased, are here,
  Where English ships once fixed their standards bold,
But not 'tis feared at times with atmosphere
  Most proper for their vogue; they, deemed too old,
Are left to lie about the bookworm's room,
Fit subjects for the negligence of gloom.

VI.

A volume worn, transcribed by scribe adept,
  The eye observed one day within a chest,
That a sea-captain had in storage kept
  For years and years as he on ocean's breast
Had voyaged to and fro; perhaps at times
To pause and read the book's engaging rhymes.

VII.

Page after page was turned—to read of eagerness
    Peculiar to thy youth; how thee imbued
With tact thy sire; of thy apparent meagreness
    Of will when facing Mæcenas; how sued
Thy city friends for news; of that bore slow,
At last from whom thee rescued Apollo.

VIII.

A rural picture soon with faithful hue
    Itself revealed; it caused in turn desire
To mingle with the represented view,
    Evoking well attention to admire,
An oaken woods upon old Roman ground,
Where depths beguiled to depths in silence bound.

IX.

Ere long the pages spread another scene,
    Holding the mind bewitched a happy date.
A Summer hour moved by; it was serene
    Like river that no bowlders agitate.
A-something in the mood a vision bore—
The Shadow-Land of Calm was near before.

X.

Absorbed, the thoughts were roused at last to see
    A place where man is classic heritor
Of ideas pure—a place wherein to be
    A spirit comes a joy to minister:
A royal road, full easy to pursue,
Led forth a world within a world to view.

XI.

About its entrance paused a guardian-hand,
   Aright to urge; its nearer presence filled
With strange surmises vain a period spanned
   With mystery; it mildly then instilled
A honey-comfort for the soul's own hive,
In barren months to keep its strength alive.

XII.

Shade shaded shade. It was a land of peace.
Roamed scores therein turned from the paltry aims
Of markets of the world, wherein increase
   The restless throngs as Mammon bold declaims—
A land of laurels partly to seclude
Great potent minds who dream in solitude.

XIII.

Light chastened light. A scene irregular
   About was. Mingled comrades, low and high,
In widespread groves; talked they in groups afar
   In sympathy conducing to affy.
A sage imparted wisdom to a class
That circling sat upon the matted grass.

XIV.

Socrates was a god above the rest.
   The soul's the mind's mind he foretells to all.
They with mild queries by and by request
   That he explain man's dim eventual Fall—
What scenes succeed its frosty dearth of days;
They dread some doom, but he this dread allays.

XV.

Plato, with parchment in his hand, stood by;
  His brow sagacious turned to thoughts akin
To excellence ; a-something in his eye
  An inner vigor marked; he seemed a twin
Of marble statue dowered with a grace
That shows a spirit depth upon its face.

XVI.

Goethe thus spoke in brief: Man often yearns
  For peace that comes from dwelling in a state
Of sweetness, truth and beauty; he discerns,
  Through worldly mists, the means that hold this fate;
A growth within attains, but it defied
Defies the means that make life's outlook wide.

XVII.

Richter serene, reclining in a shade,
  Spoke fitting words unto a humble few;
His melancholy voice gave earnest aid,
  Adjuring one, whose youth attention drew,
Not to dethrone his strength—to be in age
A slave, his passions master strife to wage.

XVIII.

Others were there whose deep philosophy
  Is found in prose, who lowly labored yet
To raise responsive manhood up to see
  A breadth the globe gives not. There, too, were met
Those bards whose virtues rare and fife-like grace
Still soothe the captains of our marching race.

XIX.

Virgil went slowly down a silent way,
  Now in a shade, now in a flood of gleam,
As if not prone his presence to betray,
  Perhaps beguiled by some part spectral dream;
Bent on seclusion, he retired anon
To write his tablet on of Acheron.

XX.

Dante sedate, on rough and devious route,
  Moved on behind as if he upward saw
A vision in the air. His lips gave out
  Vague mutterings. He seemed a priest to awe;
But there was that within his solemn mien
That courted sympathy from bosoms keen.

XXI.

Shakespeare, to whom a poet-throng deferred,
  Stood by; his fellowship kind favors gave
With triple pow'r of look, of grasp, of word—
  In gifts a king, in modesty a slave.
His central presence soon strolled off ahead,
Remained impressions courting all instead.

XXII.

Enrobed in cloth of Puritanic hue,
  Milton was gravest 'mong the grave; before
Him Wordsworth stood, exchanging view for view,
  As if to catch the fullness of his lore;
This, rich in eloquence, combined to cause
His eager hearer on and on to pause.

XXIII.

Others presided on a knoll, a heap
   With roses strewed, a bank where melody
Of brooklets babbled by, or in the deep
   Of distance—all endowed most righteously
To give repose and growth and moral store
Within the Shadow-Land of Calm before.

THE CHOICE OF ALCIDES.*

ALCIDES, once of Greece, to manhood grown,
   Still felt arouse the passions of his youth.
Hence he beheld first painted life with hues
Of brilliance false; then sober life with hues
Of reality—or pleasure's road before,
With virtue's nigh. Which to pursue a doubt
Left him no ready choice; and thus perplexed
He moved as one half-lost, solace to seek
Among shade-trees deep in a silent vale.
As thought suggested thought, his mind went through
A fruitless course. At last fatigued he gazed
About the area of the vale. It was
A day when Nature fills the atmosphere
With odors of her blooms enclosed in depths,

---

* The suggestion for this poem was found in a translation from Prodicus, a Greek poet, by Robert Lowth, an English author of distinction of the 18th Century.

Making the footsteps for their beauty search.
On such a quest, emotions to distract
From what they bore to what they wished to bear,
He saw approaching near two figures robed
In vestures feminine. The one had grace
With gravity; the other comeliness
With merriment. With stately mien the first
Impressed as having that within herself
Better than that of show without; that moved
Less admiration than respect, and more
Content than fancy's fervency. The next,
Not modest like her mate, came forth with step
Affected by the movements of her thoughts,
Unguided by true woman's tact, or depth
Of will, or finer feelings proud of what
They do aright, ashamed of what they do
Amiss. As if the other to outdo
In forwardness, she Alcides addressed.

"Alcides," uttered she, "thy dolesomeness
Cast off as thou wouldst a cloak of black
Ill-fitting thee, and come with me to lead.
What's foreign to thy nature, Oh, dislike!
Know pleasure is emotion's realm; a king
Can have no more. Joy in the senses dwells;
Encourage it to roam at liberty
In paradise of youth's desire—with youth
Brimful of wine, mid festal company,
And shouts and laughter and Apollo's strains.
Doubt comes from thought, perturbation from toil;

Cavil attends him who endeavors well;
Merit is honored most when having least;
Climb not that road of thorns and stones—renown;
A life in warfare waged hath wounds and death.
Followest thou that way or this?—this way,
My way, proceeding to tranquility,
Amid profusion proffering every sweet?
There fragrance woos as incense of the dawn;
There turtle-doves will tamely visit thee;
There fruit in falling kiss the orchard flow'rs.
Thy bed will be adorned with silks fresh-weaved,
Thy feasts will prove thee loved by maidens kind.
Secluded from the world that deeds do work
Contrary to their maker's will, the gods
Will bless suchwise as feeling once, all else
Will seem to have a void. Followest thou
My way? Alcides, come!"

      An answer made
His looks—he was subdued, and was as one
Confined within the circle of a charm.
She would have spoken more, as if to thwart
Her who was closely by composed in mien.
Standing apart since her arrival near
Within the shadow of an oak, she now
Stepped forth, the sun attending her with glimpse
By glimpse. A dignity was hers, increased
In pow'r by manners mild subserving it.
With artless aim becalmed she him perplexed,
Who would have turned from her in bashfulness.

She touched him on the arm, next held his hand,
Causing attention fixed from him to her
Due earnestness to pay.

    "List, Alcides," she said,
"To that which language has not means to show;
So subtile is its truthfulness, it fills
And animates that which is vanity
With qualities its opposite—to thought
Gives tone, to fancy will, to purpose sense;
It rouses aims related to the soul,
Reaching their fulfillment through weakness shunned.
Those of the flesh, not venial to the gods,
Are counter to true welfare, giving gifts,
Then taking forfeits. Know thou then there are
Powers of manly virtues that the gods
Confer on him who bids necessity,
With worth, approach them to receive. Zeus
Beholds thy state, and would have thee among
The favored. But disdain not means to ends:
Men foster confidence by able deeds;
Thy body's health demands strength's excellence;
Thy parent's traits in thee development;
Thy friends need counsels freely from thy lips;
The poor thy gold, the wronged thy arm to aid;
Thy country asks allegiance to her cause;
Thy race in battle use heroic feats;
The gods devotion and simplicity;—
These means to ends remotely win the prize—
'Tis proof secures the choice of sacred place.

Then bid the tempter who would thee mislead
Avaunt—her who would lead thee to a course
Contrary to existence's wiser goal."

    Alcides stepped aback from her a pace
Or so; as came conversion unto him
With sweet enlightenment, he bowed to her
As slave to mistress.

        Saw the tempter this
Askance. Attempting to conceal chagrin
In winning features, she drew near and paused.
Her sway o'er him then trying to redeem
(For knew she youth is caught by captious strains),
She spoke again:

        "Thou hast those hopes aroused,
Alcides, which forsake, like birds, fruit-trees
On which they feed; for when a danger comes
They fly, and would much rather starving die
Than living live in fear. Experience shows
That failure hath a score, success hath one;
This one, perhaps, for failure's number fit,
Yet thrives, but in his thriving hath the voice
Of envy sounding in his ears. Then know
Thy hazard in assuming what may lead
Not to the front, but to the rear. 'T is well
Before ascending to reflect that height
In pow'r, in goodness, in renown, is depth
Of shame and gloom to him who falls. Observe

With toil and trouble men purchase bright days,
Thinking them diamonds; but, alack! they fade
Like dewdrops. Then with ease, enjoyment's arts
And love awaiting thee, why tread the path
Not suited to thy youth, its hopefulness,
Its eagerness, its ecstacies? For know
Thy nature is of too refined a mould
To change itself by leaving joys behind
And meeting woes before. Then come with me,
Alcides!—Hark!—'t is music's instruments
Lulling the air afar. Let's thither go.
Come! come!—be generous to thyself, and come
To blissfulness."

           She paused. With finger fair
And glitt'ring with a ring she pointed out
Her way, then stood queen-wise, an actress through
And through. Alcides turned aloof, and moved
Athwart the grass, avoiding her with looks
As if she absent were. His reason saw
Her now; his folly when she came at first.
A false tie to the real her actions held,
Forbidding what her words desired of him,
And causing doubt to lessen confidence.

   Anon the one of modesty who had
Abashed retired, came forth, appearing now
As if she felt her cause was gained with aid
Of aught diviner than herself. 'T was thus
She spoke:— "Alcides, thy perception is

To thee a monitor that knows the tongue
Of evil. Praise to it! Then cherish it
Over thy parts immortal to control,
And to instil a sympathy for what
Makes mortals brave and great; for fare thou must
Like a hero of the antecedent times,
Bearing hardships before the guerdon came
Unto the palm, the bay unto the brow.
Life seeks its law; it otherwise is vain.
Selfishness drinks joy's wine until it cloys,
Causing a melancholy to succeed,
That to relieve itself must sport amiss,
To find, a brief while on, delusion's charms
Exhausting are. Then learn, the serious brow,
The temp'rate want, the nourished truth on truth,
The feeling warmed and beautified by hope,
The trait on trait endowing patient strength,
The attributes that quiet triumph know,
The sense combining all in character—
Its own example of compacted worth—
Rejoicings have peculiar to themselves,
Deep, deep, within the province of the soul.
Furthermore, what thou art may be the root
To show a growth which haply may produce
The fruit, celestial in its taste, relished
By gods the most. Then take the path thy mind
Foretells befitting is; directing thee
'Twill be conjunctive to thy own repose
(When to pale ashes turns thy form) within
The regions of the blessed."

         Thus ended she—
A goddess from the skies. As such revealed,
She wielded double potency that stirred
Bowed Alcides. He breathed as one who had
A second nature gained, inspiring more
Than that the first, prophetic of a meed
Awaiting him in years to be.

                    He said:
"Thou art unto my thinking part that which
My speaking part can not expression find,
O goddess! to make known. A something near
To gratitude, but which hath more than it
Of love and faith, a strange possession has,
Making me sadly glad. But let in time
My actions be on path that thou hast shown
What will thy satisfaction pay as meet
From me to thee, and be, approved by thee,
To me a consolation and a guide."

     Thus long ago he spoke to her, and was
From youthhood turned aright. Unfolding forth
The oaken quality of heroic strength,
He dropped upon the earth of human growth
The seeds of greatness. Hence when destiny
Its final shadow o'er his figure drew,
Mankind his loss perceived, and evermore
Him knew as Hercules the mighty one
In sphere devoted to the gods, himself
Empowered, co-ruling upon a throne.

THE CITY IN RUINS.

OF yore a city by Time's river stood.
    Holding commerce with silent, distant worlds,
Rich argosies came stealing from the gloom
As if from the Unknown, and bore such fruits
As mortals tasting once, love more than well
With sober hunger's yearning. There they dwelt—
A people favored by a righteousness;
By qualities of mind not of a race,
But of mankind more large, commensurate
With those of fabled deities; by types
Of beauty, all unconscious of their charm,
With virtue's spirit e'er sustaining them;
By manly tone deep in affinity
With wisdom's valor, happy in the skill
Of choosing hopes that met ambition's aim
With sweet reality.

              But to a close
An era came, like Day that sees the sun
Go down, and is in gloom. A heavy cloud
Above the city hung, and pensive was
The brow where joy had been, as oracles
A grievous time foretold. Life's modes had changed.
Succeeding on the heels of vanity,
Freedom's discord licensed oppression's ills.
Some warning voices rose and spoke of things
As once they were, and to the present turned
With scornful fingers. But, alack! men's ears

Were deaf, or whene'er otherwise not prone
So to adapt their acts unto the means
That would reform their plight. Anon there came
One who did mutter words from depths of that
Strange fervency which works within the breast
Of him who has just found fresh inner might
Accruing to the virtue of himself.
A sharpness of mild sense was his to cope
With life's sure obstacles, o'ercoming much
With kindly effort when his will arose
And bade him courage use. Often he stood
Above a crowd, as separate from it
As Nestor from a soldier-throng, resolved
And still resolving on accomplishment
Of duteous service. Speaking, men he tried
To move with new impulses, next new faiths,
To give a tenor to their lives that would
A reason for itself have in deep thoughts,
And form a project for creating well
Out of old themes, old laws, old usages
A period better for humanity.

  Once in the forum uttered he: "These days
Affect the blood and make it feverish,
Unsettling us from habits regular.
Our actions false give false results. We know
The present is a destiny wherein
Man moves forever and forever on.
Yet hope ne'er glorifies each day's events
With what it would have pass; it more observes

In what's to come than in what is, because
It sees a future measureless, that keeps
It restless by a false comparison.
Contentment, wise and charitable, invests
E'en poverty with noble sentiments,
Making lowliness good despite itself;
Giving a certain calm, apprehended
By those who are in sympathy with what
Unfolds in secret silence truth by truth.
Some conscious of this calm, do reach for it;
They blindly grope within, their store of pow'rs
Among, but find it not, in turn to feel
Emotion's ignorance is life not born
Into the freedom of a thinking world.
Thus in endeavor lost they strive. It seems
A shadow shadows them, although they are
Within the light that warms. The years both come
And go to multiply seed over seed,
Growth over growth, fruit over fruit. Nature
Produces these, but barren they. Their lives
Unfortunate in that they feel not long
The higher arts of mind which would transcend
In some forthcoming destiny—have sight
Beyond the present in perfection's cause,
Become adhesive in its earnestness,
And find in mental limitations they
Are passengers unto some distant point
Of double capability. Therein
Ambition finds its pay in noble aims,
And honor in fulfillment; for therein

Fortune is less and less; therein the weeds
Of vanity fade more and more; therein
Content increases, shining after nights
Of trouble on days of quiescence, men
To clothe with Nature's robe, they claiming her,
She claiming them; thus hand-in-hand to go
Adown the vista of successive years,
Endowed above the world's environment."

He ceased. His speech was vague to auditors,
Deeming he spoke of men remote, and not
To men anear: his tact too fine for them!
A part had called him false and turned aloof;
Others had lingered by to hear, but their
Emotions cold rose not to warmth of faith;
And others still, a few, his words had heard
With meaning foiled, their hearts intolerant.

The heavy cloud still o'er the city hung.
Appeals were vain. Gave succor not the gods;
Disdained, the trivial was worshipped more
Than they. Soon hopes, like fires unfed, died out
And spread their ashes o'er men's path. The cloud
Still hung and hung; at morn 'twas there, at eve
'Twas there—the sun obscured, the moon obscured.
'Twas like a portent in the sky, there placed
To make hearts pause and fear. For guidance men
Looked into life's abyss—no ray was seen.
Some turned to crime, and others to despair.
A misrule came by which the strong despoiled

The weak. Old placid times were never more
To be! Then suddenly, as if by awe
Inspired to flee from plague, great throngs their beds
And household gods upgathered, leaving day
By day through archways of the town,
And left its shrines, its walls, its palaces,
Its theatres to slow decay—
To solitude made grim by Ruin's hand.

DOWN AMID THE SHADOWS.

ONCE on a time at night the musings turned
    To mystery—the soul's dark covering—
Oblivious sleep—freedom from cares to have—
From struggles vain with Fate's dull malady.
The hours moved off, their missions all fulfilled,
Unto the depths of past's eternity.
At last a dream, with symbols of an art
Presenting truth, unfolded these events:

    It was the frontage of a grove whose winds
The foliaged haunt of sweet-mossed earth foretold.
A pathway ran through it to distance far;
On either side were vistas touched with charm,
As clouds o'erchanging seemed adown to send
From their own hues a tranquilizing haze.
Upon the pathway moved anon a throng
Of youths, with maidens dressed in white or red,

Who soon an open gate approached, and went
Within the Garden of Gay Sciences.
Therein the throng themselves dispersed—under
The shady silence of an oak-tree old;
Among retreats knee-deep with verdure's growth;
Under fresh bow'rs, each bearing clustered grapes
In purple plenty; by a grotto rude,
Where festal things were spread; by crystal pools,
Reflecting boughs above with sprays thereon.
The lotus and the asphodel combined,
Though opposite, to lure, each in its way,
To places proffering much of speciousness.
Thought seemed espoused to some quiescent realm
Of tempting deities, dream-webs to spin,
Enmessing self in Epicurean ease,
Believing it true life, not its sure doom.
Pleasure instilled forgetfulness: in vain
Shone down the calm religion of the sky;
The beaming hours within revolving time
Sped on unnoted through the arch of day.
Faith's ministry unfelt. In mild disdain,
There Wrong appeared to cry: "Away with creeds,
And all the jargon of the holy church,
That would restrain with Puritanic bounds,
That bids that done which doing thwarts man's pride."

When came a twilight shadow o'er the world,
As if Nature, supine, was doomed to die
Amid her plenitude, half lost in dark
The garden seemed. How transitory oft

Within contented minds the sunny hour!
As clouds above with self-mysterious pow'r
Just stirred, obscuring stars, compunction caused
A melancholy numbness of the thought;
And down a vale of doubt the footsteps moved,
Leaving the garden to deep shades of night.

   Anon was seen, approaching slowly near,
A man in hermit's garb. He held aloft
A lantern, choosing with its ray a path
That led from place to place. A cup he bore
That quivered in his aged hand. In time
He was hard by, and bid with Stoic glance
The lips partake what was within the cup—
A gall from fruitage squeezed once left to grow
Within the garden of the mind. Alas,
The draught most bitter was! Then thus he spoke:
"Conscience am I to guide to fate below."
The mystic scroll of good he then explained;
Then with stern quality of voice defined,
With counsels meet, the changes that befall
Man's growing nature, that, by Time impelled
Towards ills fronting, unavoidable,
Subdues them all, he proselyting self
To virtue from probation's course of years.
He ceased, as sighs of wind about were heard.
Then with a cold and silent dignity
He led a devious way, until a bound
Was reached, wherein a cavern's stony depth
Afforded downward aid to parts remote—

Downward through aisles—by sounding grottoes chill
With subterranean airs—through chambers wide,
Where long stalactic shapes were pendent o'er.
At last, where daylight's red and purple orb
Ne'er peered, the goal was shown. Therein
Chaos most old (Nature's ancestor grim)
Was clothed in formless solitude to reign.
Toward him went as if an innate force
Them urged a spirit-throng (and lo! it was
The self-same throng of youths with maidens that
Within the garden moved) to surrender
Themselves (each unabsolved) thereto and shades—
Yea, everlasting shades within the goal.

 As when faint sounds of discord in a dream
Alarm, appearing thus so real, so seemed
A voice to rouse the soul at waking dawn
The verity of things to understand,
As Time stood to redeem, upholding means
And crown of beauty, asking but the will
To rise and earn the treasures in his hand.

THE PLATO OF THE TOWN.

H IS intellectual being stood out large
  And bold—a giant form—on the hill-top
O'er carnal lowliness, above his kind,
And men preferred it so. A season of his years

Had come wherein he saw abundant crops
Rewarding sacrifices of labor prior;
But hopes forespent among the ills of time
At last met disappointment more and more.

    He had seen men with cynic's eye. Whilst thus,
His instinct to select mistook its way;
It chose a field perplexing—in extent
Perplexing still;—in searching for few facts,
His theories to color with belief,
A contradiction came in cognate facts,
Making his purpose feel its feebleness
Before his reason. Next impatience moved—
Moved him, the man of flesh, long-haired, rough-browed,
With ribs and thews of rare development,
As thinking wrought a spell, and cast behind
Sensations crude. Then with a sigh he looked
Upon humanity with urbane eye,
And felt at peace with it and with himself.
In course of time, his disposition changed,
He saw rare things wherefrom he formed an aim,
Having both fervor and stern confidence.
Profoundly measuring much good by good,
And finding charm in each, resolved he what
He chose into a model fit, ideal,
Austere, whereby himself to mould. Awhile
Aloof in solitude abided he,
Acquainted with the things of moral weal,
Unfolding joy in concord with the days
That consecrated were. To him it seemed

More virtues than he had could be near brought
Through thought—they in salvation were afar
Glorious in perfection! Thus he would,
Whilst still pervaded by earth's atmosphere,
Remotely haunt eternal Consciousness,
It deify, and to it kneel as to
A shrine. The present was a stepping-stone
Unto the height he saw before; the past
Absorbed him not, for yesterday was but
The edge receding of oblivious years.

With that warm trustfulness which mothers feel
For traits marked in their offspring, so sincere
He upon doctrines nursed relied, and felt
Them meet to go abroad to honor win
Through services, and bless their cause with pride
At their effect. But lo! as to and fro
Went crowds, in body much, in spirit scant,
Finding, then missing ways unto their weal,
His voice was strange, its meaning mute to ears
Adverse. He taught things counter to the world's.
No sin did he excuse, with passion's touch
In tone, suggesting egotism was moved
To countenance another's fault for sake
Of self-agreement in supporting what
Bestows authority for breaking laws
And exculpation for the consequence.
Man's greatest sin, he showed, is vanity;
And it would rather cheat to gain esteem,
Than undeceive to lose praise false; than be,

Would rather seem a long life through. It turns
To hug the false with zeal, because it serves
Expediency with a pow'r to thrive
More certain in uncertainty. Hence such
A wrong in Paul excites no self-reproof,
Perceiving that it gives him liberty
To take from others to himself: his pride
Connives at it, his habit sanctions it,
His conscience favors it with sophistry.
But such a wrong in Job arouses what
In Paul is hateful selfishness, and makes
Him loudly censure his own sin in him
More fortunate, in order not to lose
His own advantage through means of falsity.
Thus is the world confounded in its aims;
Too prone to choose the wrong and not the right,
It sows false seed, and harvests bitter grain.

  His words were laws to some, they greeting him
With deference; but others blind, who knew
No honor save that honored by the eye,
Not by the mind, would flatter him. He met
These with a mild disdain; for flattery
To him was satire hid, him showing frail
Deceived by it; for worth is full, he knew;
Content within itself, inviting none
To put a value false upon its traits
With spurious means. His censor conscience just,
In love with humbleness, at peace with all,

His mind bore fruit sustaining him, and had
A Summer in its wintery rigidness.

   But on the whole, his firm endeavors failed
Larger to make men's sight with his. He shrank
From where his neighbors gathered oft to talk,
As disappointments slowly bowed his head.
Within a tenor of a life of shade
With shade, of depth with depth, he settled down,
And faced conditions with philosophy,
Then Death himself at a mature old age
With animated confidence;—and men
Preferred it so.—'T was thus he died, and dead,
They knew him as the Plato of the town.

THE RECLUSE.

Amicus humani generis

AMONG the vales he dwelt. He knew the stars
    As seamen know them, watching through the hours;
He knew the winds, and whence their odors came,
Feeling their spectral spell; he knew the sounds
Of morn, each with a missive to his ear
Of thought and pleasure grave; he knew the world,
Judging with senses keen himself and men
At large. Acquainted with both life and death,
The latter was to him a birth, himself

In womb of Time, awaiting for death-life,
With Fate, the second nurse, expectant close.
He thus relations held unto a state
Of rarer being, doubly living high
And low, exchanging thought for thought; and hence
His sympathies enriched themselves with what
Proud apathy deemed valueless. He knew
Doubts nourish troubles more and more, and faith
Protects itself by shielding joy in hope.
Him moved convictions good and manifold,
He fearlessly upholding them. He loved
The common tenor of a common way.
His modesty—not of the borrowed sort—
It fit him like a coat most aptly made—
Touching the hearts of men, caused them to view
His nature with approving eye. Indeed,
He moved humanity with what him moved,
Leading his followers toward the lore
Revealing life's ulterior ends. He showed
That men do worship what they need: Dives'
Repast is Hunger's gospel; calves of gold
Are honored for the metal, not the form
Expressive of a moral fact; and that
Reason's purpose is folly's servant oft,
Yet seldom weaving from its discontent
The home-spun comfort of contentment.
Yet doth the soul gift them with inner light,
That once to see seems unaccountable,
Still that they know is, feeling that they are
Somehow moved by the self-same light from worse

To better. But to follow flesh man finds
A sacrifice hath been his pilgrimage:
Bearing with heavy mind increasing loads
Of knowledge false, to nature blind, he sees
Vague depths, and follows failure as a torch
To dismal loss; or by ambition urged,
He fronts the sun of fame; his shadow falls
Behind to represent him to the world
Disfigured on the stepping-stones by which
He would by slow degrees ascend. Nowise
With truth, he deems himself with knowledge rich;
Deems what appears is equal to what is;
Deems Nature's emblem is a thing to wear,
Fruitless, the lapel on of vanity,
Whilst Nature's self to conscience sighs and speaks
Of thwarted usefulness. Hence Nature casts
His shadow on the stepping-stones to show
The world his own disfigurement that is
Within himself—to Truth with truth she shows.
She leads the mind to choose earth's sentiments—
The good from bad—the wheat from chaff—and gives
Unto emotions' bounds a sweet extent,
Having the possible in chrysalis,
Enabling them to see right means, right ends;
See flesh as dust, and soul as life—see their
Own triumph after death unfolding still
Their pow'rs in an eternal secrecy,
In recognition of the truth of Truth!

Suchwise he taught unto adherents few
With systematic patience of a mind
Endowed to minister from deep belief
And bosom purified. A friend or two
Felt favors on them thrust with solemn force,
Upraising from unworthiness, yet saw
Themselves unripe in his maturity,
Meeting his presence with a seriousness
As if it were a medium sure to depths
Of Providence in visionary realms.

THE INSISTENCE OF NATURE.

<small>"Nature the vicar of the Almightie Lord."—*Chaucer.*</small>

WHAT independent life among the fields!
    The spirit of the month assuages it
With nameless calm. Withal, the air doth hold
A solemn virtue known to him who thinks
Profoundly of his being's attitude
Toward the mystery of that which is—
Of that which near in privacy of Time
Instils emotions with a sympathy
For day and all its hues, for night and all
Its orbs. The fields, the hills, the vales, the woods,
Clothed in a tranquilizing green, hath each
A potency, embodied not, yet speaks
Of hidden excellence—of something rare
Behind their folds. Approaching the ideal

Of what is better than the best within
Itself, the mind is moved. Here faith trusts life
To come, as murmurs cast a spell; deep, deep
They sink, and the imagination move,
Conducive to faith's end of happiness
Through visions seen. Within a pleasure comes
Anon to stay; it shows that Nature is
Unto the hope a language and a law,
Inspiring and directing it with dreams
Musically attuned. Thereby the sense
Is amplified with pow'r, not from within,
But from without, and with perception clear
Compares the *pro* and *con* of man. It sees
His dwelling place is darkness. Yet his night
Is neighbor to his day; his self at worst
Is neighbor to his self at best; his fate
Is neighbor to his choice; his woe to joy;
His falsity to truth; his life to time
Eternal. Death's sorceries perplexes him;
He ponders, still no sweet assurance has;
No depth in him reveals unravelment;
The offspring of experience come and die;
His energies work not in noble use;
He shifts his efforts here and there, and deems
Fortune, not Justice, will a favor grant;
In quest of Wisdom, spurns he pearls before
His feet, and gathers Folly's flow'rs. Alas!
Forsaking his divinity, he aches and mourns,
Then toils and climbs, yet scorns that altitude
Of thought which parts him from the ways of earth

And human interests involving him.
Nature at hand with scene, breeze, leaf, bloom, brook,
Bird, bee and sound, has aught for him to claim —
Association fit!—but 't is his whim to live
Within himself as in a spell adverse
To her—as in a mould imperfect made,
And not in unison with heart sincere
And mind exact. Indeed, his flesh and blood
Both foster self in selfishness. Hollow,
With Nature he endeavors to brave out
Some cause amiss—shows what he is, he is
Unknown to himself. 'T is she that knows
Him all, and for his discipline debars
Him from the grace of that intelligence
Of self until the time appropriate
For qualities abstruse; meanwhile to him,
A common man, 't is she that is a pow'r
Both when he sleeps, and when he wakes; when he
Mistakes, when he succeeds; when he obeys,
When he commands, and in uncertainty
Of change by change most certain is. Amiss
He reads transitions past from child to man;
He feels not they attain a destiny
Remotely placed. When he relinquished states
Of former growth in other ones to dwell,
Despite himself, he felt not gain from means
Awaiting his advent, nor anticipates
Those yet reserved. Still silent Nature near
Insisting, with her myriad pow'rs, unites
Him to herself, influencing him through years,

Until perfections raise themselves above
His blemishes, and calmly honor him
With virtue's thought with virtue's soul to guide.

TEMPUS FUGIT.

TIME flies! we fade! although we breathe in joy,
 Heart-fruitful in a cause of truth, in hope
The future will answer each fond desire
With palmy fullness. Winter near, we say
That harvest comes with it: with Nature's laws
At variance, faith is over-strong, and makes
A zone adapted to its purposes,
Ignoring aught besides. 'Tis thus we dwell
In joy, in hope, in faith. The past is seen,
Where wandered as the butterfly the sense
Ideal, it haunting us from year to year,
Making us dream. Somehow this feeling old
Prevails in spite of what hath been, and gives
A second soul devoted to an aim,
Not of this world, but of that world to which
As phantoms travel we with silent feet
From point to point. Still drowse too oft
We on the wayside banks, avoiding then
The background deep of sober thought, purblind
To that which only can accomplished be
Through aspiration active to its end;
And our purblindness would embody things

Not worthy of the true unfolding depth
Of life. Then melancholy comes anon,
Playing with touches strange upon the mood,
As we in it behold reflected traits
Of what ours are. With Time associate,
The subtleties of nature show what we
Could be, and urge the disposition's zeal
With greater effort to fulfill a work
Befitting, as a mould, the figure of ourselves.
Though often deaf to them, they speak to us,
Like oracles, as with authority,
As rise.we by slow heed from levels that
Depress the will's free sensibility,
To elevations that sustain and soothe,
Enriching with those means which to the sage
Reflecting deep, feels best, sees best, keeps best,
And reads the history of the human mind
With vision comprehending more and more.
Still we exist in what we feel; see things
That never were, nor will they be; in vain
We look for them, conjuring with ourselves
In spite of learning, time, eternity,
Wonders to do—play heroes to a glass;
See much in little, fail to mark what's great;
Teaching the puppet-self an aping trade,
We think each day a stage whereon to act,
And acting think the game of life is won.
The truth that animates sincerity
The heart possesses not. Our frailty seeks
Excuses for itself in fancied gifts

Of strength that fail in exercise.
Sense pines for what it hungers, leaving pass
The hour of grace for mid-day's dubious boon,
As comes a palsy-touch upon the flesh,
Making us grow old. Sentiments intense
That flowers are with aroma, that need
The warmth of happy circumstance, die ere
The fade-time; and we altered are from what
Is warm to what is cold. In coldness lost,
Too much we claim, too little others give;
Our grafted pow'rs bear other fruit than ours;
What folly feels we worship as a shrine:
The reason sees not with a lordly eye;
We solve one problem, then for thousands ask,
Them answer not, yet stand we by the one,
Deeming our insight to a greatness grown;—
But, lo! our pride is great, ourselves are small.
We find us idols to upraise, that move
Those passions secret which men aggravate,
Making them mad, misleading them from Truth—
From Truth who mirrors in themselves that fate
Which shows at last results, with something fraught
Having a choral symphony for soul
To hear in vagueness of its faculties,
And see unfolding scenes of finer joy,
And feel incentives to endeavors great,
And know reward in new experience sweet:
Yea, bliss they never breathe, within a sphere
They never reach, is there—deep, deep within
That fate. Still Time flies. Still we eat, and drink,

And sleep, and soon forget both kin and friends—
The victims of the tomb—and turn to meet
Another morrow with another face.
Still purposeless, our faith's without a heart;
Our wants mere vapor to evaporate;
Our transient mood in fellowship with scorn;
Our peace mere ashes—burned out coals
Of former action. Still we bubbles court,
Then find them gone; or hunger for the fruit
Ere days of blossom; or esteem a charm
Locked in futility. What gives to mind
A fibre firm, and gives to brows brows not
Their own, and hues to hues, and life to life—
The everlasting light of destiny—
We know not. What's nobler than ascending change!
Duty is e'er a path whereon dew-gleams
Invite before to Time's upraising grade,
Transforming life to death, and death to life
In peaceful unity with heaven's own change.
But still Time flies! Returning not with us
Again, another throng will take our place
In other seasons and with other scenes.
'Tis even now encroaching changes end
Must soon. We fade like cold November leaves;
Yet falter ere we fall, as Fate below—
What Fate?—the one of prophets true who tell
Of beauty and its righteousness remote?—
Awaits to gather to the shade of shades.

STEPPING-STONES.

I.

A YOUTH pursues a butterfly anear
   Upon a road that seems to lead to groves;
He deems a guider true the winged gaud;
He deems a journey brief toward its goal.
Anon the guider's gone, the road is lost
Within a labyrinth of forest trees;
Then sober Eve comes on to show his thought
That life's ideal is merged within the real.

II.

A youth that plays with toys by Fancy made
Dream-wise within a garden green of Spring,
Foretells where tends the footstep of the mind
To gain a manly bourne in time before:
What country it will reach to claim a tie,
What soil approach with favor to possess,
What seeds implant within the fallow ground,
What sheaves bind in the fertile harvest month,
What fruitage gather from the branch's hold,
What measures of the bounties once acquired
Others will give to help their journey on.

III.

A youth, though in a narrow limit born,
Though knowing naught of trade and far affairs,
Can with his mere imagination form

A vast domain where he alone is lord.
True laws of government he may ordain,
Rare public virtues show for models just,
Wise intercourses hold with neighbor-realms;
May build, o'erthrow with alternate design
Work to surpass before with work ere long.

IV.

A distant goal is open to be gained,
Wherein are laurel wreaths to crown success.
As ancient champions eager to outdo,
Proud youths devote themselves their will to train
To reach a prospect of bestowing years.
They turn from specious spheres wherein abound
No heights to beck them upward to exalt—
Wherein are souls that know not their great loss.

V.

The tendency of faithful Love first touched
With early gleams of its awaking light
Is to retire from ways of turmoil-trade,
To rove alone in brighter atmosphere,
To purify the mood with clearer thought,
Like a cloud that leaves the dismal folds of storm,
Seeking some tranquil sky afar to turn
Its aspect dark into a snowy one.

VI.

The alchemy of Love transmutes within
Dull dross to gold: a man in fortune thrives

Among his friends; he gains abundant land
In neighborhood of towns; keeps wolves at bay,
That haunt about a poor man's meagre means
As if in scorn of cabined poverty;
Enlarges all his views, that see afar
Life's Unities awaiting to assist
Him year by year in adding to his worth.

VII.

'Tis Love that aids the bud of knighthood out
Under the warmth of sympathetic skies,
To tinge the petals with a color known
To eyes adept in reading mystic lore—
In seeing depths under a surface lie.
Anon a bloom with symbols o'er it spread
Unto an idle, wond'ring world it shows,
Throngs to a centre of repose to woo,
Them with a lotus-touch of calm to charm,
That they may turn to dwell its sphere within.

VIII.

A woman's soul a star of guidance is!
Purblind the man her roses of delight,
Her invitations to a peaceful bower,
Her harp to hear inspired by sympathy,
Refuses, deeming them with snares replete.
She spreads around her glamour, which conceals
The bosom of her worth; it serves to woo
Unto those traits of hers that fruitful are—
That multiply themselves in men—that move

Hearts masculine, unconscious of the cause,
In sweet effects to act a lifetime out.

IX.

Let higher self desire in time to claim
A heritage from Nature fraught with traits,
To scatter them as seeds within Life's field,
The growths virtues, the fruits thick pendent o'er.
Some evils show upon the branch's form,
Others virtues in prime's copious season;
Some have the marks of folly on the rind,
Others the juice of wisdom at the core.

X.

To live awhile with things of silent Time
That are in sky, in air, on earth, in sea—
To hold communion with them all, to feel
A strange beatitude in turn arouse—
A beatitude to haunt in day, in night;
A pow'r without to rule a pow'r within
To draw life's forces forth—is to conform
The manhood to a way of rectitude
Essential to the progress of its state.

XI.

The cold may come with Winter in the front;
The stars retire behind the sable clouds;
The storm assail the tree-tops on the heights,
Ruling god-like in bold obscurity;
Still round the citadel of manhood stern

Let feet move on to utter timely cry
When danger near approaches to besiege—
Let thoughts thoughts sentinel to see
That all their duty do until the morn,
That virtues housed within may be secure,
That evils may be held at proper bay.

XII.

'Tis nobleness of thought that well inspires
Toward high purposes; these once achieved,
Prove false the fear of those that them conceive
A sacrifice to gain. A largess great
They give to all. Who turns a reason loath
Upon them shows a disposition crude—
A thing amiss, astray from its true path—
Nature within distracted from its aim—
Himself a germ devoid of helpful soil.

XIII.

A heart of charity a servant is.
It traces truth unto its secret haunts,
Discerns that periods are at service good:
The days come forth their labor to perform,
The nights have weary vigils to maintain,
The months support their burdens to the front,
The seasons serf-like push through heat or cold,
The years at work are sternly moving on.
Then why should man disdain to be confined,
As things of Nature are, in service-tasks,
That truth may well reward him in the end?

XIV.

To worship day-dreams is a tendency
Of those who love their fellow-beings well—
To cherish passing schemes the race to raise
Above normal unto supernal good.
Hence they oft labor in a fond belief
That an event encounters to oppose.
The path of progress blocked, in turn it seems
Charity's aim is doomed. Those elements
Promote that with small gain small gain improves—
An object little makes, but large in worth.
Then worship not day-dreams with their false views,
Ye charitable, but lowly labor on.

XV.

A man of wisdom sees rare things before,
Mystic at first, yet at a future hour
Clearer they show themselves; they footsteps lead,
As indexes, to golden eventide—
That eventide of time where Age at ease
Sits down among his sundry records old
To read his past—the fortunate release
From days once tangled in a web of years—
The new-come freedom—happiness restored—
The spirit mounting o'er the flesh to find
Its sum of troubles but a brief ado.

XVI.

A vista clear before of thought profound
Presents a goodly prospect all the year—

No Winter rash pours down with Boreal breath
A frigid fury on the fleeing South.
True effort means a journey to its bounds —
A task confined within a course of time,
That self-adjusts unto forthcoming ties,
It knowing they bestow due recompense.

XVII.

The pow'r to bear a judgment firm on self,
To prove its faults, and censure so the same
That they repeated cause to conscience pain;
To prove its merits, raise them to a place
That they become reminders, each a form,
By which to aid the spirit-faculties;—
Is oft denied to those that callous are;
Absorbed in specious things spread out before,
They see within not their own dormant gifts.

XVIII.

A life of mere cold years wherein to move
As one confined upon an island lone,
To eat, to clothe, to sleep—no more—is dross
Surrounding gold—a seed within a rock—
The Real opposing the Ideal, that needs
Warm years, a hemisphere of space, the looks
Of love, the social sympathies of homes,
And temples which contribute mysteries
Imagination to arouse.

XIX.

The voice of inner truth holds converse with
A world of shade, of light: the one has death,
The other life. Life has a force to go,
If no defects retard, through far degrees
Of light, growth to assist in endless space.
Then carry self from flesh to criticise,
As in a glass, the flaws upon the soul
That it may to due remedies apply.

XX.

In existence there is a bounty rare
Greater than Himalaya's bulky range,
Whereby the heathen swart in fancy sees
Of grandeur tier on tier to uplands high—
A bounty that beyond succeeds itself
In settlements most firm of rising ridge
O'er ridge, until the outline of a peak
Stands forth, a crown of white upon its brow.

SLEEP.

THE harvest-field of dreams is poppied o'er;
    Within deep sleep we reach the highest peace;
The warmth of Summer gives a bounteous rest,
With calm's enchantment in its atmosphere;
Then let us turn to slumber, turn to dreams
And their vague spell. Now is our harvest stored,

How sweet the song of labor done and past!
Yet mortals need a self-forgetfulness.
Change comes by law, and not by chance, and gives
Something better for something worse. Follows
Attainment after toil, life after birth,
Death after life. Involved in change, we have
Our longings, and would with the birds rejoice,
That sing in happiness unconsciously;
Seeking it not, it comes to them at will;
With us 'tis otherwise. Our seeking foils
The search, or finding cloys the sympathy,
And leaves amiss what would appropriate be,
With disappointment ever in the fore.
Then slumber we, and dream, forgetting ties
Of earth, cobwebbed awhile in gloom of glooms,
Akin to blessedness of night, and warm
Like Lethe's stream, assuaging in its sound
Upon the pebbles; dead to thought and strife,
To heart's triumph, to mind's environment
On some Parnassian height of laurels won.
With plain food by we hunger for a feast;
With feelings moved we see with erring eyes;
With common gifts we would transcend the gods—
Yea, dead to these, ambition's heritage,
Let's lie in slumber, deep within ourselves,
Whilst to our spirit comes, on mission sent,
The starlight's spirit from the twinkling gloom,
Making us placid evermore in years—
Placid and wise like silver gray of age.

OLD AGE.

OLD AGE! what are to thee the airs of youth?
    The roses on the cheek of joyousness?
The supple gait in concord with a will
Of inward animation? Health and bliss
Bestow their charms, then leave behind a taste
That profits by their loss, inspiring thought
With precepts fitted to the mind's fond wont
Made grave by years. Thy melancholy's cold
Hath then a heat engendering growth of fruit,
Hanging between the branches of thy gnarled
And crooked strength, with flavor that
Commends itself. Yet men sit at thy feet,
As at an altar, fearing thee too prone.
Thy Roman look hath awe compelling them
To shrink. They hear thy wiser words as words,
With inner meaning e'er devoid; thy board,
With viands set, mixed simple needs, are scraps
(The penalties of begging poverty)
To them; thy actions are construed to fit
The understanding that doth censure thee
Amiss in cold dislike, or serve a jest
To subjects that dilate themselves in terms
Hilarious about the tavern door,
That mimic heedless of the consequence.
Yet thou, too, wert as they—thy scoffing time!
Then thou hadst fancies wild—just as have they!—
And love unsettling thee, and frolics oft

Within the town! Strange crotchets, too, thou hadst
In aims, a score by score, which never found
An issue in fruition! Then quaint ideas
(That opposition taught thee how to guard
With words of prejudice, withal sincere)
Of spheres remote from thee, whose habitants
Were paragons for men of politics,
Where justice law forestalled (in theory!)
Where life a tenor oped to vistas rare
Of intellectual fields—of wisdom's life
The form, of patience's life the soul. It thus
Appears a spirit in thee worked to show
To where all tend, and made thee dwell at times
In spheres befitting to the use of what
Within thee is, and by comparison
Of good with bad led thee from change to change—
From worst to best in semblance. Life's rare worth
Lies in obscurity. It crowns hairs gray.
'Tis thus a royalty becoming thee
Favors thy state—proud privilege above
Thy kind! From the beginning to the end
Thou seest men distinguished from the paths
Wherein they follow leaderships unseen
To fancied points unseen—with pity's eye
Thou seest. Thus Xerxes saw the movement vast
Of multitudes in whom survival's check,
He knew, too well, was the green turf on which
They trod—the earth that bore them would reclaim
Them dead. Where then the music of their tones?
Where then each beauty and its sorcery?

Where then pre-eminence with honors cloyed,
Yet, selfish, reaching out for more?—But ere
The leveling time doth come, unto thyself
Austere, who speaketh little, thinketh more,
Prevaileth thou like a magician skilled,
Discreet, in weaving into thy strange web
Of destiny such colors of thyself
As make it strong and beautiful; and in
The furrows of thy years the seed is cast,
To garner when the month of harvest comes
Sheaves of thy pow'rs, ere Autumn seals with cold;—
And thou art blessed, Old Age!

BEAUTY.

'TIS Beauty that makes music to the march
    Of life, and makes men feel as victors ere
A victory's won. She doth inspire that which
We know not of, but which emotions mould
Into an apprehension rare, and make
It strong and confident; and of that which
Doth harmonize with peace, until it makes
The territory of our happiness
Extend so far it heaven seems to meet
In horizontal calm.

            Inhabits she
The sky, the earth, the sea, the breast of man,

With aught attuned to poesy in all
Her moods, profound yet simple in her means
Well used, as fleeting as the rainbow's tints;
As tranquil as the trees of tropic woods;
As changeful as the billows of deep seas;
As lasting as immortal spirit, where
Purposes flourish, bearing seed and fruit.
Turning melancholy to hopefulness,
Her presence's ever felt but never seen.

Her own salvation is enduring truth;
Infusing it into choice Nature's works,
Unfolds she them into a vital form,
Its color virtue, and its odor soul,
And gives new glory to old worldly things.
In meadow's haze upon a warm June day
Of themes romantic to artistic minds
She speaks, as if behind a golden veil,
With language deep from her intuition keen.

Ling'ring by the shore of idleness,
Praying that Triton may, as once of yore,
Blow his shell-trumpet, giving earnestness
Unto our frames that we may go abroad
To vanquish in accordance with that which
Holds beau-ideals of what heroic is,
We think of Beauty, Aphrodite's birth,
And thinking, dream with double pleasure evermore.

AURORA.

AURORA, thou with man must sympathize;
I deem that love is in thy light; it comes
Adown the East on slopes dew-spangled o'er,
As if a dove from heaven's lofty haunt.
If so—for otherwise how could it be?—
A certain knowledge of the truth would give
Fresh life, fresh faith, fresh aims unto my mind
Of maiden thoughts. Sojourning here below
Awhile, birth comes but once, we pause a term,
Then wander through the gloom to thee. 'T is thus
On Roman soil I breathe and hear the flow
Of Tiber ever in my ear, and so
My feelings flow within the channel small
Of present sense, and wish for bounds more wide.
Meanwhile, I consecrate myself to thee,
To live, to hope, to have secluded joys
And blithely to attune my inner self
To tranquility. When the woods are green,
The fields adorned with blooms as red as wine,
The brooklets sprightliest with Summer sounds,
Then seems a special benediction comes
From thee to me. There's alchemy within
Thy presence, turning dross to gold. The Earth
Feels it with buoyancy; for lo! she knows
Thou comest to bestow that which makes rich
Her o'er and o'er—yea, richer far than all
We know of Elysium, she dowered is,
Making the gods with envy look at her.

Then, too, beholding upward at an hour
When clouds besprinkle rain upon the hill,
They glow, approaching thee, as if they sent
Strange incense from a shrine to thee supreme;
And when the rainbow steals athwart, it is
Thy glory; and it is felicity
To deem Æolus lulls his winds awhile
To murmur music to thy ear. No less
Is fancy moved (for fancy doth create
What it loves best) to deem, when harvest days
Come with their Southern warmth, Ceres uplifts
Her features potent with expressiveness,
Observing for awhile with kindling eyes,
As if with rapture mute, next turns to praise
Thee for thy silver store inspiring that
To grow which is her cherishment. Then, too,
Pomona mild, among thy gifts the flow'rs,
List'ning serenely to the chirp that comes
From near some ærial nest by branches borne,
As if a lucid spirit spoke to her
Of innocence. Slowly she treads, nor heeds
The thorns that would her peplus tear; busy,
As is her wont, she finds repose in toil,
And dreams in harmony with mellow hours
That woo her grapes to ripen. Flushed her cheek;
With intuitions years have amplified
She Nature reads, discerning what instils
The mind with traits not native to itself,
But are adapted from the sphere of spheres.
Hence she through Nature feels the motherhood

Of light, of warmth, of life with super-sense
(That in our language human lacks the means
Of speech divine), and on thee, Aurora, looks
With a reverential concern. —If meet
For both a goddess and a nymph to see
Thee thus, how well in beings less to pay
Oblation from the temple of themselves,
That would amend and elevate ideas
From earth to heaven, there to find thee still,
E'er ceaseless in thy blissfulness, and feel
Impressions high rewarding moral pains!
Ah, me! thy blissfulness supernal, e'er
In youthfulness! Ah, me! there's mysticism
Confronting with its outlines ominous,
And backs would rather faces be, and scan
Past's light than future's dark—uncertainty
To come, the which to meet, we creatures frail
Excite belief with a false faith to keep
Life's purpose roused. Withal, pure consciousness
Ennobles our desires. Turning to thee,
A sweetness and a patience in thyself
Assure somehow of favors yet to come
From thee—not echoes of mere joys, but joys
Themselves unto the mood enamoring—
And soothes contentment anxiety o'er fate.—
Thy spell Tithonus felt; requesting life
Of thee, he dwelt within a change by law,
Yet not exempted from the change himself,
He reached age old, with it decline. Then long
He moaned, as one in darkness cast and held,

Unto the distant light of fabled isles,
Bearing decrepid limbs with wrinkles bound,
His woe not youth perpetual. He witnessed
In dawn's streaked gray bewild'ring to child's eyes,
Thy sunny locks and smiling countenance,
Thy beauty and alacrity, whilst pouring dew
And spreading flow'rs as emblems of thyself—
Unchanged in peerless radiance (but, Oh!
Him seeing, and deploring him!) thou wert
The type of what he wished to be, but, ah!
Was not! Still it appears thy heart's own fires,
Celestial-kindled at the hearth of Time,
Must have in far reserves for him and us
(Immortals proving with due worth) that which
Inspires in part with what thou art thyself.

ADVERSITY.

DO fragile blooms, o'ercome by midnight storm,
   Retire to grieve when rains assail their form?
Does Spring grow pale when checked by Time to know
She cannot beauteous Summer's path down go?
Ah, no!—the blooms the cruel drops perfume,
And Spring robes Time from her adorning loom.
Why is it, man, that thou art false and frail
When Fate debars or daunts thy days assail?

FATE AND PROPHECY.

WHEN hoary Autumn spreads upon the mould
    Loose leaves of russet mixed with streaks of gold,
Grim Boreas, god-like, blows South a cloud,
As trees in sudden pangs do moan aloud.
Will words of omen waive the course of things—
Deny that Summer warm, on zephry wings,
Will give calm joy to counterpoise this bale?
Ah, Fate will prove those words an aimless tale.

MAY.

I.

WITHIN a hall are placed a rare display
    Of prints of nymphs and graces known of old;
Some with thought strive, others with fancy play;
    One by a niche impresses once beheld,
Showing a Queen's bygone pastoral throne,
As broken roses are about her strown.

II.

A woman's beauty is upon her face;
    The spirit's dignity still lingers there;
Three lambs beside her one another chase
    Each moment's happiness surcharged to share,

As rests a shepherd on a mossy mound,
Breathing quaint harmony's Arcadian sound.

III.

Beside him near some meadow blooms invite
  Admiration with dewy splendor mute;
Under them close, within a leaf-wrought night,
  Are belle-formed buds, each robed within a suit
Of finery, all breathing Lydian air,
That would have him Pan-like to linger there.

IV.

His life not vexed by dull or dolesome cares;
  His peace perpetual, free from battle-harm;
His friendship's sympathies not knowing snares;
  His bosom's depth afire with love's warm charm!—
Oh, could his notes be heard, thus honor May,
Who from her Southern zone comes forth to-day!

THE SYBARITE.

I.

LET him in a mountain home
  List to mid-day-buzzing,
  List to water rushing,
Breathe the airs that mildly, mildly roam,
    Scented with the gathered flowery treasure
    From the golden glens of ideal pleasure.

II.

Let calm Summer after Spring
    Rule this sphere of green
    With a queenly mien,
Hygeia by her side well-stored to bring
    Scarlet colors to the cheek, akin
    To a peacefulness ensouled within.

III.

Let the frontage of a villa
    View in prospects wide
    Beauty glorified—
Dales and fields of bobbing clover gay,
    As the tinkling bells of kine emerge
    From the distant hill-top's beck'ning verge.

IV.

Let beguiling butterflies
    (Each with color bright
    Like a spangled sprite)
Ramble 'mong non-seeming entities;
    And the lords of maiden roses, bees,
    Lull their loves to sleep with more than human ease.

V.

Let him in a bow'r outspread,
    Crowned with clustered shapes
    Of empurpled grapes,
Feel the coming South, unheralded,
    Breathe on thicket-buds her path before,
    Them unfolding hanging frailly o'er.

VI.

Let him hearken to a song,
   With a tone endowed
   Rare of music loud
(Such as Echo's voice could ne'er prolong),
   And a flow of fragile-throated words
   From a choir of tropic-pluméd birds.

VII.

Let him hie, O goal, to thee—
   Far from civic-sound,
   Hie to grandeur round—
There to dwell awhile, nor fail to see
   Things of hope that well the fancies please,
   Like a dream-born realm o'er dream-born seas.

THE BIRTH OF VENUS.

I.

BEHOLD the sea! a distant shape appears
   Within a cloudlet fading from the view,
As if to seek the morn's exalted spheres
   To clothe itself with their cerulean hue;
   Ere long with outlines fixed, in mist seen through,
The shape becomes distinct, and overhead
Æolus tunes his harp and symphonies are spread.

II.

Behold again! It is a mermaid queen
  Just slowly leaving her secluded home
Of coral walls, submerged with drowsy green,
  As by it sea-blooms grow. At will to roam,
  She moves upon the free, unstable foam
(As by her feet dolphins and nereids swim),
After a night, perhaps, of spectral dreamings dim.

III.

Her movements on the deep induce surprises;
  Gladly would knowledge learn the mystery
That round her throws a glamour of surmises;
  Full strange as aught that in fore-ages be
  Appears this form emerging from the sea,
Decked with red dulse, to flutter to and fro,
To stand with human weight, yet not sink downward low.

IV.

Ah, no!—not human she! What impulse high
  Upon her brow pours an affluent part
Like vesper orb! What pow'rs occult apply
  Their sorcery, so pregnant with a heart,
  To rule her countenance! O peerless Art,
Couldst thou on canvas large, in colors bold,
Once let the pond'ring mind her being true behold!

V.

Observe!—a goddess now appears she there.
  The surges o'er where maketh sun-sheen tender
A chaster glow, she rises up in air,

Impearled about and robed in humid splendor—
What graceful movements wields her figure slender!
Once more observe—she fades in height away.
Alack! what speculation could her bourn portray?

POMONA.

I.

POMONA known of old
    Among the citron groves, the purple swell
Of grapes, the wholesome olives manifold,
Hast thou denied coy-like thy wondrous spell
    This our fair Western World of freedom's hold

II.

Ah, no!—thou art anear.
Nor Greece nor Rome with its climatic might
    Could well compare with what thy fruitage-year
Pours down before Nature's admiring sight
    Upon the landscapes of this hemisphere.

III.

Forthwith behold around:
What ranged profusion! What resplendent sway!
    The tree crowned hills triumphant o'er the ground
Where valley verdure shows a like display
    Of myriad treasures that in buds abound!

IV.

She with discerning hand
Has caused each growth its blossoms to unfold—

The brimming sap well upward to expand
To reach betime the coming apples gold—
  Rich clustered globes within a pendent land!

V.

What wealth to her foreseen
Will be in August days of honey-bees,
  Hived by the blooms in drowsy orchards green,
Where she in umbrage may command a breeze
  Offspring odors from their warm mothers wean!

VI.

O happy birds, indeed!
Among gay blossoms on surrounding trees,
  Craving ere formed on cherries lush to feed!
O happy birds so careless in your ease!
  Melodious prophets of your Summer need!

VII.

Be ye but mouths to chant
To her some sober phrases from each heart;
  Her magnify with fancy jubilant;
Next let her dwell before, like work of art
  In ideal musings, e'er in dreams extant.

VIII.

'T is well for you to deem
That she is mystic, like Queen Mab of yore;
  That she prevails within each silent scheme
Of ancient mystery that hues fruit-store
  .For you, divulging gloss o'er streaks of gleam.

MY LADY.

I.

MY Lady rules supreme. Her golden reign
    Is where mild Summer haunts from year to year;
  Indeed, it is a half-seraphic sphere.
There birds sing joy's immaculate refrain
Her lattice by her daily heed to gain;
    There bees, on tribute bent, in hives anear
    Store comb by comb of honey fresh and clear;
There Nature (loyal subject she) pours grain
From harvest fields into her granary—
  In fact, all wealth is hers that Fortune holds.
But this is dross placed by her sympathy,
Imbued with woman's classic potency,
    That oft men's moods with sternest thoughts embolds.
Therefore, 'tis meet to cry, "Long live, Your Majesty!"

II.

My lady plays a lute within a bower.
  What strange excelling harmony hereby
    That moves throughout the garden! Not to sigh
Inclines with weary drooping form each flower,
But stands as if inspired by some warm shower.
    Two turtle-doves their flying wings apply
    About her person, eager to espy
Her seated 'mong green leaves a queen of power.
Thou harmony bear forth thy spirit life!
  Thy tones are fraught with meaning to impress

With truer traits of courage than are rife
   When feast-hummed music breathes at night excess;
Yet they her well denote above heart-strife —
   A thing of peace enthroned in loveliness.

III.

My Lady lives within a scene of bliss:
   A Paradise within a Southern zone;
   A simple bow'r established for her throne
Among rare roses that each other kiss;
Where all things seem endowed with that and this
   To tinge deep senses with a dreamy tone;
   Where calm eternal is with force unknown
To aid grim Time in his ancient service.
My Lady has a pow'r somewhat akin
   To that of Time among her roses rare;
Though less her might, yet her meek features win
   Bold breasts of men to find a secret there,
That makes a Paradise themselves within,
   They gaining from this source life's golden share.

IV.

My Lady is a being crowned among
   Transcendent things within an Aidenn goal,
   And to them she's at times a guardian soul
(Like Flora of the grove), with mystic tongue
To minister to wants of blossoms young.
   Their life's her life, so subtile to control
   Their virtures till they form a part, then whole
Of her enchantment all about her sprung.
But she the hearts of strong-limbed men doth sway

With art as fine.   They feel her touch, and know
The source whence she's inspired; they to her pay
　　A homage with their manhood all aglow,
And on her shrine a wreath of laurel lay,
　　Nor care from her in worldly ways to go.

V.

The pow'r that animates My Lady's face,
　　Madonna-like, contains a-something rare
　　Preferable to arts of courteous care,
Which oft denote a false or borrowed grace.
When she is on her throne above our race
　　Her words are pregnant with deep wisdom's share,
　　Leading each hearer calmly unaware
Up step by step to Life's Platonic place.
Hence hope conceives a final blessedness
　　From thought of her.   She law creates within
　　That are as ties to make the heart akin
To her pure soul.   O heart! move on no less
That earth's dark roads are crooked to excess,
　　By her high Life's Platonic place to win.

AT SEA.

I.

COMRADES, upon the deep, not shoreward now;
　　It is a port where Life and Death e'er meet;
Oh, let our vessel veer with idle prow!
　　Let worms feed there—the harvest is replete.

II.

Things time-worn have their exit over-soon;
    Then why should we aflush with labor doom
Ouselves to shore ere prime of afternoon?
    Let naught of youthful zeal our day consume.

III.

Heed not the tide that becks toward the shore;
    It shines like rolling shields of silver hue;
'Tis a decoy, the fancy vexed to store
    With images destructive to pursue.

IV.

Rather stay here and drowse upon the flow,
    Where move the demon dangers round in stealth,
Where hungry sharks now seek in depths below
    The drowned man's bones among his rock-wrecked wealth.

V.

Let us pause long. There's virtue borne by men
    That mocks at haste. Let some supernal boon,
As off our days retire and come again,
    Thought's movements to a pleasure slow attune.

VI.

Or let our pilot there, with pagan heart,
    The Present make a god, to be beguiled
To follow luck where'er it may impart
    Rare harmony from some Æolian wild.

VII.

With petrel wings we'll pass the haunting storm,
  We'll breathe equator air, know tropic calms,
We'll anchor by the coral islet's form,
  We'll feel the joy of wondrous Southern calms.

VIII.

No struggles weary-wise that may give bane;
  Life's systems fall below their models rare;
Why seek the depths or heights with turmoils vain?
  Why seek the night when day is everywhere?

THE CAGED BIRD.

I.

WHAT yearnings vain and emulative fire
    Thy tones express!
Thou wouldst gain mountain heights with pure desire
  ·The pilgrim's soul in valley of distress
    To bathe with flood of sound of warmest tenderness;

II.

Or maiden lone, love lurking in her eyes,
  ·   Busy with dreams,
Whose spell supreme conducts romantic-wise
  To realms remote, where life's commingling streams,
    In currents deep and clear, have wondrous gleams o'er
        gleams;

III.

Or youth within his thought's broad solitude,
    To broodings prone,
Yet with ambition's longings stern imbued,
    Renown to reach, hill-dwelling and alone,
    Who beckons him to climb with loud triumphant tone.

IV.

Poor foolish bird!—thou dupe to wretched fancies!—
    If thou wert free
Thy cherishings would die as do June's pansies—
    Too soon thy fervid music broken be,
    Like mermaid melody in a chaotic sea.

V.

Then let repining cease, voluble bird!
    More bitter seem
Thy thoughts than draughts from quassia-cup—they curd
    The outward flow of flattery—to deem
    Thee without full desert prevents a full esteem.

VI.

Lightly arise to sing of happy things —
    Life's charities.
With harmony's impulse well know the springs
    Of vital force and of effective ease,
    But e'er, like Apollo's lute, have a tone please.

VII.

Let not thy spirit's false forebodings see
    Fate that alarms;

Though a prisoner, yet king-thoughted be,
Thy realm To-morrow, free from gorgon-harms,
Full to the brilliant verge of Time's selected charms

THE ROYAL ROAD.

I.

A WINDING road conducts down to a glen,
    About whose sides some cavern depths allure
With hall-like passages, wherein the ken
    Beholds a smoothness for the footsteps sure;
Conducts by vines and shrubs with vivid dyes,
To fields that fill the mind with strange surmise.

II.

Here soil's rare plants in true succession reign;
    Here damask-roses court the roaming breeze;
Here rock-formed hollows show a mineral vein;
    Here spread profusion tempts the hand to seize;
Onward lead paths, paved with a pebbly mass,
To growths of shade as fresh as April grass.

III.

Seat of enjoyment, of serenity!
    You hold the few who shepherd-like adore
The guidance of supernal mystery;
    Who know so well what pathway to explore;
Who lead their flocks, on wholesome pasture bent,
To hilly heights where naught is imminent.

IV.

You hold the few who seek the Summer reign
  Of warmth and growth; you well extend an aid
To mortals prone to seek superior gain,
  Which elevates above the haunting shade
Of brick-and-mortar towns; no busy days
Impose their troubles in their divers ways.

V.

Here Virtue is demure; there's Health, whose hair
  Sports round enduring blushes; near is Hope,
With secret presence in her wizard air;
  Patience reclines upon a mossy slope,
And now she reads absorbed, and now she dozes;
Some are beguiled as humor them disposes.

VI.

Here Youth, imbrowned with tan, moves quickly by;
  Enters Manhood Wisdom's secluded cell;
Energy near is ready forth to hie;
  Courage before leads to a rugged dell;
And patriarchal Age, his dame beside,
Goes to and fro—contentment typified!

VII.

Possesses each a vista clear before;
  Each knows to use those boons by Time bestowed:
Each summons up his courage to explore
  The broad Beyond upon the Royal Road
Of earth, with purposes which generate
A love of calm, of truth, of final fate.

THE APPIAN WAY.

I.

THE Way eternal is; though some remote
    Consider it—not so!—in every sphere
It is, combining with itself the note
    Of song above with sense of what is here,
To help thought up to noblest altitude,
To find that peopled deemed a solitude.

II.

The Way leads forward through an arbored aisle
    Of bearing vines, whose stems are decked with fruit
Worthy a king's choice flasket; where to while
    Their hours oft vintagers resort when hoot
Grave owls; when Night, shade-mantled, comes to mourn
About the hills with mellow-noted horn.

III.

The Dawn beholds a few who tread the Way,
    Their heed engaged upon a point on high
They've heard of oft, and certain to display
    Outlines at last consoling to the eye.
So on they push, hardships to undergo,
Their end to gain, as summits o'er them glow.

IV.

Index-boards here and there, with festoons wrought
    Into arising verdant coils, up guide;
As hill-born brooklets, with their sparkles fraught,

Spread forth mild flowage that down channels glide;
A high flamingo flies, in scarlet furled,
As if emerging from dim Afric's world.

v.

Still upward leads the Way. The airy hall
  Of Morn no equal has for such a life!
From concord-breathing glens issues a call
  And tells of sylvan bounds with shepherds rife;
Next sounds commingle far, and mildly roll
Like spirit-joys proceeding to a goal.

vi.

Delay not near that hillock green and trim
  Briefly to recognize those buds serene;
They to much worth espoused conceive a whim
  To shy from sight and be as things unseen;
But yonder push to that excelling seat
With other hours than man's from yore replete.

vii.

There's calm about within an area vast
  To make the bosom with reflections glow
Most fit to form impressions to outlast
  Mere musings of a moment's come and go;
A calm to plant those sterling traits within
That rise until to stable strength akin.

viii.

There are events combined with sober day
  In solitude among deep forest boughs,

Where spirits seem to hover and delay,
   To murmur of a now that Time endows;
To bid ambition forthwith know repose—
Body and soul their opposition close.

IX.

There wayfarers remain ; averse they feel
   Unto experience prior, most prone to press
Them from those earnest studies that reveal
   The latitude of higher consciousness—
A succor pleasing, seen of that without
Which them contrived to keep in years of doubt.

THE STATUE.

I.

UPON a worldly highway was a stone
   Of marble smooth that long forgotten lay.
The Winter frigid claimed it for its own,
   Impressing blots for Time to wash away;
   The Summer torrid, with a fickle sway,
Blew rain or dust upon it noon by noon
Until it seemed a corse denied a burial boon.

II.

Great throngs of people journeyed to and fro:
   Philosophers with wisdom in their mien;
Merchants, some scowling, others all aglow;

Soldiers off duty, easy and serene;
Heroes, statesmen, each with ambition keen;
Lawyers, artists, scholars; beggars beside
Bankers and nobles spurring horses eager-eyed.

III.

In all this multitude not one down cast
   A look of sympathy upon the stone;
It was a relic from a distant past
     Endowed with form, although but slightly shown
     (Like a body with a soul to beauty prone),
For Art to shape unto a semblance new
That would suggest to man an ideal meaning true.

IV.

A youth demure of penetrative strain
   Beheld the marble pariah. His breast,
Exalted by ambition's wise disdain
     Of hours misused, long felt its plight unblest;
     Next schemes and dreams disturbed his nights of rest;
He strived for strength to wrestle from its doom
A monitory form a mission to assume.

V.

At last, surrounded by a doubting tribe,
   He wrought with chisel-chippings on the stone;
Advisements held he often to imbibe
     From purest elements of self a tone
     To mark the image with a seeming own
Of goodness, beauty, united to a charm,
To woo a busy world from evil's mighty harm.

VI.

Time after time he labored at his task;
  Denied himself the pleasures of the throng,
As some, perhaps with gibes, would stop to ask
    Pointless questions, next smile and deem him wrong;
    His earnest will was adequately strong,
Nor swerved a day—most like a growing oak
That firmly stood when stormy mock'ries o'er it broke.

VII.

Behold! a shape at last was there in view;
  A figure formed from strokes of firmest will;
It seemed a being noble through and through—
    A something rare to waken and to thrill
    With face benign, and fitted to instil
Deep tongueless thoughts with dialect of art
Well known to those who speak the language of the heart.

VIII.

Anon a square pedestal he contrived;
  Beside its base minutest germs were strown,
That grew to buds and next as flowers thrived;
    And then the form he heaved with brawny skill
    Up to its place superior on a hill;
Around the whole a guardian hedge was thrown,
Watchful to prick with thorns the reckless finger-bone.

IX.

He next upon the smooth pedestal cut,
  "Una!" that all the people might behold
  Through it one whom they had to slavery put:

A maid unworthy of their ways of gold—
A doe within a boa's devouring fold—
A head downcast—a voice to utter wce—
A door unhinged to creak, world-winds assailed it so.

X.

The statue, standing by the highway wide,
  With right extended arm directed feet
Toward a narrow road diverging, spied
  Afar connected with a cool retreat,
  Where laurels rose about a temple's seat;
Where deep recesses near denoted life,
Secure from din, with wholesome fruitage rife.

XI.

There day by day to point pale Una stood,
  As on her gleams descended from the blue;
There night by night, dimmed by vicissitude
  (For thunder-storms hid stars and off withdrew),
  The flow of life she sought with effort true
To move from gloom a sunshine to attain—
To roll in channels right to seek truth's main.

XII.

The multitude, oft mingling to and fro,
  With curious ken the noble figure viewed;
With steps indifferent some faltered, though
  They with its meaning failed to be imbued;
  The mass went to a city murky-hued;
Yet none, alas! unto the temple near,
Its green repose amid an Eden atmosphere.

XIII.

From a wilderness afar a demon came,
  By Una grinned a dismal hour or more,
Until she seemed to tremble through her frame,
  Hence to his goal his awkward aspect bore.
  In turn an angel from the azure o'er
Came meekly down, and in her shadow shed
A tear of condolence before she homeward sped.

XIV.

The youth, now grown to manhood prime, retired
  To spend his days within the temple nigh,
To dedicate himself to moods inspired;
  Leaving the statue in neglect, to lie
  A cumbrous ruin stretched the highway by—
Its pieces vain confusedly at large,
An easy prey for Age of burial means in charge.

THE ISLAND.

I.

APART from worldly schemes that often mar,
  Or give ambition but a passing shade;
Apart from plights that noble aims debar,
  And leave self low self higher to degrade:
O'er such supreme the Fancy, prone to roam,
Now leads to limits formed for souls who turn from home.

An isle it is within a foreign sphere,
   Enriched by Truth; where Goodness has all day,
Where Evil has no night. To deem it near
   'Tis ease, and strange beguilement to portray—
This air-born picture coming slowly to instil,
With sheen touched o'er not native to art's human skill.

II.

There is a meadow with a river by;
   Cygnets and water-fowls move to and fro;
Barges and barks with silken sails supply
   Beguiling rides as odored breezes blow,
As vestal Echo to the ear affords,
From rocky bourns remote, her sylvan-sounding words.

There are smooth paths of shade beside the stream;
   These scholars screen who turn to banks to muse;
Or converse hold in groups on some apt theme;
   Or to light ways inclined a number choose
To watch the cygnets on the current slow
Kissing the eddies clear that to their bosoms flow.

III.

There is a grove whose verdure low and high
   Shelters the feathered nest from noontide glows.
The many hymns of birds address the sky;
   How happy-throated the harmony flows!
The Day ensouled the inspiration feels,
And throbs as does a nun when she to prayer steals.

Here flowers wild in bushy settlement
  Regal affairs conduct in courtly state;
But some with eyes idolatrous upbent
  Implore a shade above, as if of late
A juggling god within a cloud of gold
Had rained down magic hues their petals to unfold.

IV.

Thickets of palm excel with smooth retreats;
  Near orange groves their golden fruitage drop;
Hedges of figs unmask their seeded sweets;
  Stand trees in rows, each has a burdened prop,
O'er which hang blossoms white, and fall below
Into the lap of earth, like flakes of Autumn snow.

Vineyards abound where grapes from coverts peep
  Each cluster rare immures the coming wine;
It yearns to break the purple walls, to leap
  Into bright bowls, and gayly to combine
Itself with noise, joyance and festal song,
To charm the palate with its spirit keen and strong.

V.

A road leads here and there. The distant ways
  Are broadly spread. The bees their sweets imbibe
Within the girdle of a valley's maze,
  Where butterflies, a Gypsy, careless tribe,
Range in the circle of an ærial calm,
Free from urchin ardor pursuing to impalm.

A field within the vale bears bearded corn;
. Another oaks, where plays with music true
A brook about a bank, on which adorn
   The azure cups of buds bedecked with dew,
Or blooms most bright, there dropped by hand unseen
Of warm-breathed South when once she faltered o'er the scene.

VI.

Beyond are forest-trees aflush with life;
   The sun appears them calmly to observe.
Within their shades what subtile airs are rife!—
   An indescribable, unique reserve—
A mysterious instinct of earth that clothes
Itself in robes of green encrowned with heaven's glows.

It is a forest huge—a choice supreme,
   In which a Diana might hap to ride
At noon upon a steed out-breathing steam;
   Or blow her horn; or deem that were beside
The hamadryads—deem that they her viewing
Would pallid turn forthwith, their envy her pursuing.

VII.

Another spot is gained. See hedges old
   Where osiers bear their heavy burdens well;
Hear torrent-murmurs far, all downward rolled,
   That mingle with the tinkles of a bell;
Mark offspring mounts, evoking sweet surprise,
Some seen with humble huts arranged companion-wise.

The smoke arises from those moss-roofed haunts.
  There dwell those who in routines rural go;
They breathe and wonder, knowing not the daunts
  Of spendthrift hopes that men impov'rish so;
On homebred things they daily place their mind,
And bid to civil arts their eyes be half-purblind.

VIII.

Anon is seen a youth hard by a tree;
  He wields a pipe; within his meadow-sphere
He pours a tone of happy harmony.
  By him five lambs are subjects of his cheer;
They move aloof, their strength to exercise,
But backward come ere long his sounds to idolize.

Hard by a garden choice of mixed perfumes
  Invites a maiden form to move around
Its labyrinths; she gleans rare crimson blooms
  And weaves them into wreaths. Something profound
Upon her brow depicts pure thoughts within,
And speaks of her as one to tender things akin.

IX.

Beside a road well sheltered from the heat,
  By rows of ancient oaks, with passive air,
A marble lion is; between its feet
  A lamb reposes—lo! a happy pair!
A chiseled figure crowned with heaven's rays,
Whereon the hand of Age no Vandal mark displays.

A fane not far is by thick laurel shades;
　There Priestess Peace imparts her truth to guide;
A composure demure within her aids
　To hold each one a student at her side;
Her speech as potent is; both join to give
A store of thoughts that eke, once eked show how to live.

X.

A group stands where the fane its shadow throws;
　Their features grave are with expressions fraught;
They talk of wealth, of Time's most true repose,
　Of worldly goods with wasted efforts bought,
Of specious hopes that urge aspiring man
His life's allotted date with restless years to span.

Yet hold they that a pow'r, although not known,
　Upward from birth deep minds to aid surround,
Infusing day by day a dreamy tone,
　That moves each one to something vague, profound,
Whereby he may sojourn in castles rare,
In foreign regions true, yet naught material there.

XI.

Nestling within a glen ascending back
　To mountain roads and wild and lofty seats,
A little town is by a shoreward track;
　Here house near house confronts three broad-laid streets,
Where sailors dwell, a stern and humble class,
Who half their rugged years upon the ocean pass.

Sea-fowls contend with wind and water, prone
  To bathe their feathers in a briny bay;
Agile and reckless, pleasure is their own,
  Nor do they it abuse with vain delay,
But homeward hie betime among cliffs bare,
Where climbing vines alone approach their refuge rare.

XII.

Throw forth the gaze afar above the wave,
  Where mullets gay and golden fishes roam;
Where sea-nympths once upswelled ('t is said) to lave
  Their hair's redundance in the hoary foam;
An eager fleet now comes, with gathered might
From balmy winds, to reach this island of delight.

Between small isles, on which are cypress spires,
  They come, emerging from a current wide,
From a great world of dearth and foiled desires,
  That strips men bare of all aspiring pride;
Where motley throngs of anxious people go
Confusedly around a huge, delusive show.

BEFORE AND AFTER THE VOYAGE.

I.

MY argosy, go seek strange Fortune's main;
  There in far voyage hail an island shore;
There let thy crew the island depths explore,
In earth's deep mine dislodge bright golden grain

Wherewith to forge a pure, encircling chain;
  Oh, bring me furthermore a floral store
  (Such as Pomona meek might half adore),
Nice silks, quaint gauds and fruits of hybrid strain.
Well would each largess charm Olivia dear.
  My argosy, hence of fresh sails make sure;
  Prepare repelling dangers to endure—
Surges' uproar at daybreak lacking cheer.
  But what are daunts by treasures to procure
With which to grace her form without a peer?

II.

My argosy's come home. What freight of ore!
  What silks produced with craftsman's choicest skill!
  What tropic blooms impressing with a thrill!
What fruits out-blushing fabled ones of yore!
Olivia fair, the sail these homeward bore
  That thou mightst turn their service to thy will,
  Yet be to all a sceptred presence still,
Ruling with grace thy kingdom spreading more.
But after all, this wealth seems not designed
  To give meet setting to thy woman's worth;
And, too, appears at times the motive blind
  That would deck thee with what by thee is dearth;
For so endowed thy beauty and thy mind
  They simply move the world—'t was so from birth.

THE END.

www.ingramcontent.com/pod-product-compliance
Lightning Source LLC
Chambersburg PA
CBHW031405160426
43196CB00007B/911